PILGRIMS

On the Camino de Santiago

Paul Stutzman

All scripture quoted from the Holy Bible, New International Version®, NIV ®. Copyright© 1973, 1978, 1984, 2011 by Biblica, Inc.™ Used by permission of Zondervan. All rights reserved worldwide.

Formerly published as a segment of *Stuck in the Weeds*

Copyright © 2021 Wandering Home Books
All rights reserved. No part of this publication may be reproduced, stored in a retrieval system or transmitted, in any form, or by any means, electronic, mechanical, photocopying, recording, or otherwise, without the prior permission of the publisher.

ISBN 13: 978-0-9998874-7-9

To my fellow pilgrims

whose hearts were also set on pilgrimage

I dedicate this book.

Lori, Aoife, Helen, Kat, Kristen, Bob, Ed, Neils, Maria, Alexandria, Teresa, Liz, Angelina, Debbie Anne, Martin, Father Jorge, Father Mike, Jamie, Christine, Judit, Martin, Ben, Ziggy, Nancy, Damien, Beth, Alice, and Maria.

I laughed, talked, and cried my way across mountains and valleys. I could have completed this pilgrimage alone, but meeting these fellow pilgrims made the journey more complete.

TABLE OF CONTENTS

Pilgrims 3

Passport to The Way 12

Vanishing Mist 20

Ancient Roncesvalles 29

Disciples 37

Basque Country 46

Pamplona 55

Winds Across the Way 63

Lightening Up 69

New Faces 75

Black-Sheep Follower 83

Choice 91

A Healthy Kind of Nuts 96

Together on the Path 100

Taking up my Cross 108

Church Chickens 113

Doors 120

Beauty in His Cathedral 128

Sunflowers on the Meseta 135

T-roads 142

Transformation 149

A Cathedral and a Simple Life 161
A Sunday's Walk 166
Learning to Believe 173
Life in a Ghost Town 178
Into the Mountains 182
Little Santiago 187
Over the Pass 191
91, Again 196
Galicia 200
A Little Rain 204
Santiago in Sight 210
Compostela 215
To the End of the Earth 223
Finisterre 230
Muxia 233
Pilgrim Communion 237
Bones Dead and Alive 244
After the Camino 249

Forewarning and Thanks

Please note that this account of my Camino walk appeared previously, combined with the Mississippi River misery and published as the first edition of *Stuck in the Weeds*. We have separated the two adventures. *Mississippi Misadventure* recounts my kayaking attempt, and this book, *Pilgrims*, follows my hike of the Camino de Santiago in Spain.

As with my other adventures on the Appalachian Trail *(Hiking Through)*, my bicycle ride across the country *(Biking Across America)*, and my attempt to kayak the Mississippi River *(Mississippi Misadventure)*, on this pilgrimage across the mountains and plains of Spain, I tried to be aware of what I believed God was revealing to me.

Some folks are very offended when biblical truths enter into the conversation. Perhaps the reason for this lies in that word *truth*. Therefore, consider yourself warned. This tome presents realities that have the potential to get one unstuck from a mundane life and perhaps send a soul off on a pilgrimage to a better place.

Thank you to my editor, Elaine Starner, for turning my thoughts and ramblings into readable form.

To see additional photos of my adventures, you are welcome to visit my website at www.paulstutzman.com.

You can also visit me on Facebook at Paul Stutzman Author for updates and random musings.

Blessed are those

who have set their hearts on pilgrimage.

Adapted from Psalm 84:5

1
Pilgrims

Outside the window of our bus, a brilliant flash of lightning illuminated the French countryside. Gusts of wind and sheets of driving rain buffeted our coach as it slowly ascended the Pyrenees Mountains.

Lori, seated next to me, looked a bit stunned. Just a few moments ago, she had expressed her thankfulness that at least the weather was good and we weren't enduring the downpours that had soaked our stay in Paris. Now we were driving through a monsoon.

I dared to utter a sarcastic remark that at least it wasn't hailing.

On that cue, hailstones pelted the coach with a savage ferocity that slowed our progress to a crawl. Lori and I looked at each other. Our situation seemed so dire, all we could do was laugh. Other passengers stared uncomfortably. Were these two hikers on the edge of hysteria? What could possibly be so funny about the horrible storm raging outside? The other travelers on the bus did not and could not know that I had once again gotten myself into a predicament.

This seemed to be happening with far too much frequency in the past few years. It was on that very day a year before that I had found myself in another precarious situation on a Mississippi River kayak trip. Why did I keep getting into these tight spots?

One contributing factor was my lack of planning. I acknowledge that. Nevertheless, I frequently deem planning unnecessary and boring. Then there was also a lack of communication, especially essential communication. I have a tendency of not grasping the "essential" quality of certain communication until that lack of "essential" communication has wreaked its havoc. The current situation was caused by a bit of both factors. My usual habit, when I found myself in a bleak situation, was to place all the blame on cancer—but I was beginning to suspect that the statute of limitations on that excuse had run out.

The fact was that I had taken a risk and it had landed me here, on a coach buffeted by a storm in the Pyrenees, seated beside Lori, a nurse half my age.

Two years before, at a book signing in Florida, a young lady I had never met before approached my table. Lori had read my book about hiking the Appalachian Trail and had been inspired to make the same hike. She had quit her job as a nurse with no promise of getting it back and set off to thru-hike the AT. That, my friends, is my kind of risk taker.

We chatted for some time, sharing our recollections of the Trail. I asked her that fateful question.

"Have you ever heard of that trail in Spain called the Camino de Santiago?"

I had often read about the Camino, also known as the Way of Saint James. I had no idea at the time who this St. James guy was or what claim to fame he might have.

"Yes, I've heard of it." She had just recently seen *The Way*, a movie with a storyline set on the Camino, and she seemed quite intrigued by that trail as well.

"Do you have any interest in hiking it someday?" I asked. She'd have to save some money first, she said, but she would certainly be interested—unless, of course, she got married first. Deeply in love, she expected a marriage proposal in the very near future.

Two years passed, during which I lived through a few other adventures and misadventures, and in May of 2014, I determined to hike that famous trail in Spain. Looking for a hiking partner, I searched through my phone contacts and fired off a text to the young lady in Florida. On my phone, I punched out only seven short words: *Does the Camino ever come to mind?*

Within the hour came a reply: *Almost every day.*

In a few days, Lori had worked out a two-month leave of absence from her workplace, and the date was set. I coordinated my schedule. We would meet up at a hostel in

Paris known as a launching spot for the Camino and then begin the hike together. Lori also made plans to connect with two hikers from Germany that she had met on her previous Appalachian Trail hike. Her friends would arrive at the Paris hostel at the same time we did.

Lori's dream was to hike the Camino from France through Spain, finishing in Santiago, the official end of the Camino. In Santiago, her boyfriend would meet her, propose marriage, and together the two of them would leave for Germany and Holland for another month of adventure.

Oh, how even the best plans can go awry. Just before Lori's departure for Europe, her hoped-for fiancé broke up with her, and she flew across the ocean to Paris in a sea of tears.

We would actually start our hike in St. Jean Pied De Port, a town nestled in the foothills of the Pyrenees Mountains in France. Two trains ran from Paris to St. Jean. The first train was scheduled to arrive in St. Jean relatively early in the afternoon. Any hiker on that train would have ample time to secure lodging at a hostel in town. Unfortunately, we had not considered that August is holiday time in Europe, and virtually everyone is on the go for the entire month. The early train from Paris to St. Jean was completely booked.

A later train heading to Bayonne was also booked but had two standby tickets available. Lori and I stood by, and, fortunately, managed to board that train. In Bayonne, we waited for another train to take us closer to St. Jean, our destination for that night.

While we waited, we struck up conversation with other hikers also heading to St. Jean. One young lady from Australia had taken off an entire year and was traveling around the world. Another traveler was Aoife, a 22-year-old Irish girl also on holiday and planning to walk the Camino. Her lilting accent was music to my ears. A young man from London, with a Cockney accent so strong as to make it a foreign language, struggled with his overstocked backpack. His grandmother had previously hiked the entire Camino and had loved it, and he believed if Grandma could do it, he could as well. I observed his heavy boots and inquired if he planned to hike in them. He did indeed. Silently, so as not to offend the unprepared youth, I mused that if he persisted in dragging those clodhoppers along at the end of his legs, he would never get over the first set of mountains.

We heard from a few hikers that beds in St. Jean were at a premium and perhaps even sold out. A few phone calls made to the hostels in the town confirmed that fact. I wasn't too concerned about this situation, though, because I knew Lori had a three-person tent scrunched up in her backpack.

The tent was only a backup plan. We had determined to stay at the hostels along the trail, the *albergues* reserved for hikers on the Camino. Some of the albergues offer private rooms, but most have large, communal areas with thirty to one hundred beds, sometimes stacked three high. Beds in the albergues are rented out on a first-come, first-served basis, for a price ranging from €10 (10 euros) to €15, the equivalent of about $14 to $20 per night.

We knew, though, that the albergues fill up quickly. A tent might be useful, should we be shut out some afternoon. So, in our planning process, we had formed a contingency plan. A text conversation between Ohio and Florida had gone something like this:

LORI: Were you thinking of bringing a tent to camp?

PAUL: I was planning to use the hostels as much as possible.

LORI: I have a three-person tent I'm bringing.

And at this reply, I proceeded to make assumptions and based my own plans on those assumptions.

Wow, a three-person tent, I had thought. *That's the equivalent of bringing a three-ring Ringling Brothers and Barnum and Bailey circus tent.* You see, I'd stayed in a two-person tent on my Appalachian Trail hike, and that tent had been spacious enough to shelter myself and all my gear. A three-person tent would be quite adequate for the two of us and our backpacks.

Before you start questioning the wisdom of a man sleeping in a tent with a lady half his age, let me assure you of one thing. This was only a matter of convenience. Why drag two tents along when one will do? Following a grueling day, hiking partners share a tent for one purpose: to catch much-needed sleep. For many days to come, I spent my nights in albergues with ladies sleeping in cots left and right, closer even than two people in a three-person tent.

(Hopefully that has allayed any suspicions of devious behavior some of you might have had. Don't try to kid me—I know some of you did.)

So while we waited at the train station in Bayonne, we talked about the possibility that we might have to camp that night. I was not concerned. We had our backup plan. Lori had a three-person tent.

The train arrived, we boarded and were on our way again. This train ordinarily rolled all the way to St. Jean, but the railroad company was doing maintenance on the tracks, and so we were again deposited at a station where we boarded a bus for the last leg to our final destination. We had spent the entire day traveling from Paris, and our arrival now would be close to 11:00pm.

At least, it wasn't raining. Our short stay in Paris had been dampened by downpours, and now, faced with the probability that we'd be camping that night, this was one thing to be thankful for—no rain.

Lori had voiced that thought, and in a matter of minutes lightning flashed, the wind picked up, and rivers coursed down the windows of the bus.

Aoife's musical accent was heavy with concern—she, too, had not made lodging reservations in St. Jean and had no idea where she would be resting her pretty Irish head that night. On a rainy, dark night in an unfamiliar town, she had no place to sleep or even take shelter.

I reassured her. Little Miss Lori had had the foresight to bring a three-person tent, and thus far, only the two of us were scheduled guests that night.

In spite of my gallant offer, I admit I was getting a bit anxious. This might be a little crowded. Would I be the thorn between the roses?

About this time, the light of knowledge dawned upon Lori. "You didn't bring your tent?" she asked me.

"No, of course not. Why would I, with you bringing a three-person tent?"

The light was beginning to dawn for me, too. There seems to have been some miscommunication here. When I agreed that sleeping in a tent might be okay occasionally, Lori understood that to mean that I would bring my tent and she would bring hers. Seriously? You have a three-person tent, and you think I'd bring my own? Ridiculous!

"You said you were okay with sleeping in a tent," said Lori.

"Yes, I was okay with that—sleeping in yours. Your three-person tent."

"But... but..." Lori was stammering, and I knew this was not going to be good news. "That tent had a rip in it and I sent it in to be repaired. So I brought my one-person tent."

This was a predicament somewhat of my own making, I admit, but I wasn't alone in the dilemma. Beside me, a young lady alternated between crying brokenheartedly and laughing hysterically, and she was here because I had invited her into the adventure.

I tried to assume practical objectivity as I contemplated our sleeping arrangement and Aoife's distress. I suppose if we were attempting to get two people into a one-person tent, we might be able to cramp three in there. But I was pretty sure I would be the odd man out—out in the cold and rain.

"At least it's not hailing," I remarked to Lori, putting forth a small offering of comfort.

That's when we heard ice pellets begin to pound the roof of the coach.

The bus eventually arrived at the train station in St. Jean. Weary hikers picked up their backpacks, stepped down to the street, and slowly vanished in the quiet, darkened town. Clodhopper boy clopped away to his hostel without so much as inviting us three to share his bunk.

A gypsy with long frizzy hair and his stick-thin lady companion picked up their guitar and shabby belongings and ambled off as well. His cat perched on his head. That creature, at least, had a place to sleep that night.

The bus roared off, leaving us three bedraggled strangers alone in the parking lot.

2

Passport to The Way

I had taken a risk, and it had brought me here, to an unfamiliar town, standing in a dark parking lot with two young women, and no roof over our heads for the night. The red taillights of the bus disappeared in the distance, and the dark streets seemed inscrutable.

Most of the hikers who had disembarked from the bus hiked off with the sure knowledge that a warm cot awaited them somewhere. The three of us who had lacked a bit of initial planning simply chose a street and headed off into the darkness, in search of hospitality of any kind.

We heard the commotion of shouts and laughter coming from a building ahead of us. As we neared this watering hole dispensing spirits of an earthly nature, we also saw an inn across the street. A large, black iron gate at the street guarded access to the inn, but we opened it and walked into the dimly lit lobby. Not a soul was in sight. We rang the little bell on the desk, and the proprietor appeared. What a relief to discover that he would be happy to exchange one of his vacant rooms for €30.

The room was very large and very warm. I pulled back the interior shutters, intending to open the windows to catch any possible breeze that might be passing through, and discovered that our room also had a view—right across the street to the noisy bar, where we could see patrons engaged in or cheering on rowdy matches of arm wrestling.

A better view looked out over the tiled rooftops of St. Jean Pied de Port, toward the Pyrenees Mountains, now only dark shapes rising into the night sky above the town. In the morning, we'd see the green fields and forests on the mountainsides, and we'd walk over those crests—as we began our hike to the end of the earth.

Many hikers started out early the next morning; some even headed up the Pyrenees Mountains before dawn. Lori, Aoife, and I had a late start. Until the wee hours of the morning, we had been kept awake by the boisterous, drunken partying across the street.

Our first goal was to seek out the pilgrims' office in the old, historic part of St. Jean. The streets are narrow and cobbled and at places cross arched bridges over the River Nive, which runs through the town. Parts of the wall that once surrounded the medieval village still stand, now surrounded by later additions to the town. We walked through an arch in that wall and followed an ancient street to the pilgrims' office, the official check-in point for walkers starting their hike in St. Jean. Here in this old section of town, many buildings have been converted to inns or albergues catering to the pilgrims who have come from all over the world to walk the trail known as the Camino de Santiago.

At the pilgrims' office, we received information about the first part of our hike, were given weather reports, and obtained our passports. These are not the typical passports used to travel from country to country, but rather a small booklet known as the *credencial del peregrino* (pilgrims' credential). I was a pilgrim, and this *credencial* booklet would document the walk I was about to undertake. Hostels, restaurants, monasteries, and churches in the Camino network all have their own unique stamps with which they mark each pilgrim's passport as he travels through. Pilgrims are awarded a certificate of completion at the end of the trail only if they can present a passport filled with stamps as proof they've walked the route. The certificate of completion, or *compostela*, is a much-desired document. It's not only a personal confirmation of an endeavor undertaken and finished, but also a respected recommendation when seeking employment.

The trail we would follow over the Pyrenees into and across Spain to the end of the earth is called *el Camino de Santiago*. *Camino* is the Spanish word for *path* or *way*, and *Santiago* derives from *santo* ("saint") combined with a form of

Yago or *Iago*, both with roots that go back to the Hebrew for *Jacob* and translated as *James* in our English language. This ancient path is often referred to simply as "the Camino" or "the Way of Saint James." There are actually many other starting points for the Camino across the Iberian Peninsula, all eventually merging, but St. Jean is the beginning of what is known as *Camino Francés*, beginning in this little town in France and crossing the Pyrenees Mountains into Spain.

When I determined to take this hike, I knew very little about who St. James was or why this route would be named for him. What I did know was that people have been walking this trail for over a thousand years, it was almost 500 miles long, and it was a famous Catholic pilgrimage.

Each year, approximately 150,000 people attempt to walk at least a portion of the Camino de Santiago. What compels folks—hikers, non-hikers, and all degrees of those between—to commit weeks and even months to a walk over mountains and plains?

Bones.

In medieval days, the pilgrimage started when one crossed his own threshold and left his home. No matter where one starts, the goal is the Cathedral of Santiago de Compostela, where, in a silver coffin, lie the bones of an apostle of Jesus.

Yes, my friends, bones. Or, more accurately, *relics*.

Now, I know that to many of you a relic is an old car, possibly resting up on blocks and rusting away. The old jalopy the Beverly Hillbillies drove could be labeled a relic. For most of my life, the term *relic* was rarely used, and—when it was uttered, it most often pertained to just such a pile of dilapidated machinery.

But my definition of *relic* was too narrow. I know that now. Perhaps to some folks it even bordered on the sacrilegious. I know that also. This immediately shines our spotlight on the strange elephant lumbering about in the room, a peculiar and unexpected situation which, you will soon see for yourselves, creates an opportunity for you to extend to me a good dose of grace. I will surely need it as we journey together.

You see, I was a Mennonite pilgrim in pursuit of relics and miracles on a very Catholic trail.

Fortunately, I was not denied a passport because of my religious heritage. Nor was Lori, who came to this trail from a Mormon background. The Camino accepts all who wish to walk the route. Those who believe in the power of the Camino trust that miracles take place, no matter who you are. All are welcome—Catholics and non-Catholics, atheists and believers, scoundrels and saints, Mennonites and Mormons.

As I began to learn about the apostle who inspired this walk and the deeply spiritual significance of the pilgrimage, I saw that to really make sense of it all, one needs a sense of Biblical history, a vivid imagination, and faith—lots of faith.

I know the Biblical history.

I confess to nurturing, even cherishing, a vivid imagination.

And faith? It's what I build my life upon.

But a Mennonite walking a Catholic pilgrimage? As I said, I hope you'll extend me a generous portion of grace.

As you know, I'm a hiker. Hiking is good for you. It gets the blood pumping. I always feel that a good hike gets much more blood to my brain than hours of just about any other activity. There is something about wilderness hikes—you and nature, alone together, with you carrying everything necessary for survival in a pack on your back. Long ago, I discovered that nature has a soothing effect. God must have given us the beauty of the world as a natural relaxant and healing agent.

After I've been on the trail awhile, I reach an amazing place. Not a destination, but a mental, emotional, and spiritual place. Perhaps it's also physical. I'm walking along, and *nothing* is happening. I call it flatlining. I'm sure my senses perceive my surroundings on the trail and my mind is probably doing some processing, but I feel no stress. I've shed the worries and puzzles of life. It's just me and my hiking sticks, clicking along, a part of God's good creation. *Everything's okay.*

So how did this Mennonite come to be hiking a Catholic pilgrimage trail in France and Spain? Part of it was certainly the call of adventure. I needed adventure. Most men do, once in a while. A factor might also have been that I'm now in my sixties, and I'm making an assessment of the way in which I am using the numbered days that still remain for me.

During my many years as a restaurant manager, I worked all day, week after week. At the end of the month, I'd get a profit and loss statement. I could actually see what my effort had accomplished. Now, in my new life as a writer pursuing adventure, things like *success, results, achievement,* and *productivity* are very difficult to measure. There are days that feel as though I've done nothing. I may reply to emails, sit down and force myself to squeeze out a few words on the computer, meet with someone, or perhaps speak in the evening at a gathering of some sort. But sometimes I feel as though my hours are just *gone*, and I've lost entire days I will never get back.

I had been thinking more and more about legacy. What am I going to leave behind when I depart for another city, a perfect city where I will take up residence? Even more important, what am I sending ahead? Anything we do here, now, has results in eternity.

Am I doing enough? Am I where God wants me to be? If I'm a follower of Jesus, what *should* I be doing? And although I claim to be a follower of Jesus, I was beginning to wonder if I even know exactly what that means. I felt as though I was just as stuck in the weeds as I had been in the Mississippi River swamps, not quite certain which way to take forward and maybe even paddling in circles.

As a hiking enthusiast, I had read about the Camino for years. The decision to walk this trail was an impulse—at least, that's the way it came to me. I was out walking one day, with my hiking sticks clicking along but my mind and body restless. The Camino and my conversation with that young woman in Florida came to mind. I stopped right there, on a country road, searched for Lori's phone number and sent her a text.

At that moment, I was conscious only of the desire to go walking again. But looking back, perhaps the Holy Spirit was stirring the undercurrents of all the thoughts and questions that had been growing in my mind. Just as the Spirit helps us when we don't even have words to pray, He also helps us when we need to take steps forward but have no idea how or in what direction to move.

At the pilgrim office, we received the first stamp on our passports. We were also directed to a basket full of scallop shells; for a donation, we could choose whichever of the fluted, delicately-colored fan shapes appealed to us. We each tied one to our backpacks, following the first of many Camino traditions. The shell or scallop has become a symbol of the pilgrim on the Camino. Many people sew them onto their clothing or wear them around their necks.

A shell you ask? Be patient. We had such a late start—it was now almost nine o'clock and hundreds of pilgrims had already set out ahead of us—and we still had not eaten breakfast. My feet were ready for the Pyrenees. The story of the scallop will come in due time.

At a small café we bought pastries and coffee and sat on the steps outside while we ate, watching pilgrims go by, all heading out of town. As with the start of every journey, I wondered which of these people I might meet again on the trail. What conversations would lead to friendships? What experiences would I share with them? What would I learn?

Then we picked up our packs and our Camino walk began. It was a Sunday morning, and as we neared an old stone arch that had once been a gateway into the city, we passed a church and music drifted out to meet us. I went up to the front door and listened a bit. But I did not linger long. It was as though the music was drawing us into our pilgrimage. We passed under the arch, crossed over the river, and began an uphill climb that would lead us over the Pyrenees.

3

Vanishing Mist

Two routes cross the Pyrenees, both accepted Camino paths. I carried a popular guidebook, *A Pilgrim's Guide to the Camino de Santiago,* by John Brierley. The guide divides the Camino walk into 33 daily stages (one day for each year of Jesus' life) and includes maps and descriptions of terrain, information on lodging and eateries, and directions to significant historical and spiritual sites along the way.

The guidebook describes the choices of routes between St. Jean and Roncesvalles. The easier route threads along the lower foothills through wooded areas, often running parallel to the main road. This route was the shorter of the two.

The more arduous way goes up and over the Pyrenees. The path winds steeply up the mountainsides, up and up and up.

This route was the choice of the French emperor Napoleon, when he moved his troops in and out of Spain. Medieval pilgrims also preferred this path to avoid bandits that often lurked along the wooded lower roads. The high road over the mountain would be more challenging, and the guidebook cautions that before making this choice, one should consider both the weather conditions and one's own physical condition.

The two options reminded me of the decision we must make about the path we take in life—either the broad or the narrow way. The broad way is the easier; many people choose that path. The narrow way takes more effort, more strength, more endurance, and more determination. The only problem with this comparison was that the two routes over the mountains ended up at the same place—which is not the case for our choice of paths in life.

We chose the high road, called the *Route de Napoléon*. The day was gorgeous, with white clouds drifting through a blue sky. Most of the uphill climb was paved, a narrow asphalt roadway with crumbling edges and barely wide enough for two cars to pass. Fortunately, only a few cars traveled the road.

Our legs and lungs were soon aching, but spectacular views rewarded us. Behind us, we could see St. Jean at the foot of the mountain. In the valleys, other little towns huddled together. A patchwork of green fields interspersed with wooded areas covered the mountainsides and reminded me of the farming country at home.

This mountain hike was nothing like the mountain climbs on the Appalachian Trail. For one thing, the Smokies and the Whites we climbed on the AT were often thickly forested with none of the pastoral scenes here in the Pyrenees. Another difference was the difficulty of the climb. Although this stretch over the mountains between France and Spain is one of the toughest parts of the Camino, it was not as difficult as the climbs on the Appalachian Trail.

Nevertheless, this start to the Camino is exhausting for many people. That included me. As usual, I was not in the greatest shape when I started this hike, and Lori and Aoife sprinted out ahead of me. I settled into my own pace, enjoying the views.

After 5.5 kilometers—every step of it upward—we came to the first albergue along the trail. The building also housed a restaurant and bar. The hostel offers 22 pilgrim beds and several private rooms, and many people make a reservation here for their first night on the Camino. We were committed to ending our day at Roncesvalles, over the border in the Spanish province of Navarra, still about 19.5 kilometers away, so we stopped only for water and a short rest and then walked on.

We had about 12 miles to Roncesvalles. Europeans, of course, think in kilometers, and the signage is in kilometers. When I read signs, my mind automatically converted the kilometers to miles, since I've been conditioned to gauge distance in that way, but as I grew accustomed to walking in Spain, I found I enjoyed using that measurement—kilometers are shorter than miles, and I could knock off ten kilometers faster than I could hike ten miles.

The road kept going up. As we climbed higher, we left the wooded areas behind. Sheep, cows, and horses grazed freely on the slopes. Almost ten more kilometers brought us to a wayside cross, a symbol that we saw many times each day along the Camino. I'm sure there's a story behind every cross erected along the trail. Who built it there? What prompted them to erect it? For the spiritual pilgrim, the crosses serve as constant reminders that no matter what it is we're seeking, our answers are grounded in truths represented by that cross.

Here, the trail left the asphalt road and turned onto a graveled byway. Waymarks on the Camino are yellow arrows indicating which direction the Camino turns. The arrows might be on buildings, stones, trees, even the pavement. Frequently there is also a sign with a modern schematic of a scallop shell, usually yellow on a blue background.

The arrows pointing the way for pilgrims are a recent addition to the Camino. In the 1980s, a Spanish priest who believed in the importance of the pilgrimage trail took up the project himself, painting arrows along the Camino all the way across Spain.

To my amazement, we met Clodhopper Boy on our trek over the mountains. I admit I was surprised he had made it this far. For a time, he tried to keep up with me, but I was working to keep up with Lori and Aoife. They were ahead of me, and since I was out of shape, walking fast enough to keep them in sight had me gasping and wheezing. I knew the young man wanted to stick close to us. I didn't blame him. But if I slowed my pace to stay with him, I'd lose my hiking partners.

It wasn't that I felt compelled to stay with Lori and Aoife for the sake of companionship. I often enjoyed hiking alone, and there were many times we were hiking with other people. But I did feel somewhat responsible for Lori. She was a capable and independent adult, and she had thru-hiked the long and arduous Appalachian Trail, much tougher than the Camino. Yet I knew she was here because of my invitation, and, in addition, she was going through a tough time, grieving the loss of a dream. I watched over her like a father.

Finally I made a suggestion to the young man struggling along behind me, "Go at your own pace. Take your time. Take a rest when you need it. There's an albergue coming up. You might want to consider stopping there for the day."

He finally sat down beside the road, looking forlorn and lonely. That was the last time I saw him.

That happens at times. You meet other pilgrims, hike with them a while, maybe even have dinner and stay at the same hostel that night. And then you never see them again. Others, you may cross paths with frequently over the course of 500 miles. Some become lifelong friends.

I also met Bob and Kristen for the first time that day. A father and daughter team from Idaho, they instantly caught my attention because Kristen was carrying both backpacks, one in front of her and one on her back. Bob had injured his back and was unable to carry his own pack. We struck up a conversation when they spotted the AT patch on my pack and surmised that I was a fellow American.

The gravel road dwindled to a small dirt lane with grass growing in the middle. It was a way for walkers only. No cars were permitted.

We stopped at a spring to replenish our water supply. A stone structure had been built into a grassy hillside to channel the water through a spigot. Inscribed on the stone were the words *Fontaine de Roland*. We would hear more about Sir Roland later. He met his demise somewhere on this mountain or the valley below—accounts of the battle vary. Stone benches at the base of the slope offered a welcome rest. There are many such water sources along the Camino and in the small towns, and throughout the entire trek I never felt it necessary to filter my drinking water.

Our path now looked something like a field lane at home in farming country. We even came to a cattle guard placed in the lane. And once we walked across, we were officially in Spain, in the province of Navarra. That's how easy it was to go from Basque France into Basque Spain. Only a stone marker alongside the dirt road indicated that we were now in a different country.

Although the name *Basque* refers to a specific section of Spain, it also refers to a larger region where the people share a common culture and language. The Basque people reside in both northern Spain and northwestern France, and rather than refer to themselves as "Spanish" or "French," they insist they are "Basque." The cultural unity of the entire Basque region transcends arbitrary lines drawn between countries. Various groups, both militant and political, are working to gain independence. In 2004, the Basque parliament declared that the region had a right to secede from Spain. This triggered an ongoing debate and power struggle between the Spanish government and the Basques who say they are not under the rule of Madrid.

The dirt road now sloped more gently upwards, and we eventually reached the top of the mountain where we had a glimpse of the town in the foothills below us. The monastery at Roncesvalles would be our destination for the night.

When the road turned to the right and we were finally headed down toward the town, Aoife turned into a rabbit. She was in great shape and took off, leaving both Lori and I in the dust and arriving in town an hour before either of us. She paid dearly for her haste, though. Blisters covered her feet in the next few days. To our advantage, the blisters did slow her down a bit.

I also picked up speed. Downhills can be more dangerous than climbing, and they're tough for most folks, but I enjoy them. My hiking sticks and body click into a reckless sort of rhythm and I'm like a blaze, headed for town. That's not sound hiking advice, I admit—only a quirk of my own style.

Lori had been ahead of me for the entire day, but now I passed her.

We were hiking along the side of the mountain, through a magnificent beech forest. Looking down the path ahead of me, I saw a mist drifting through the trees. It was nothing like the morning mists at home that hang in the valleys, nor like a summer fog we sometimes encounter when driving. This misty body moved through the trees like a quiet creature of the forest.

"Lori! Get down here and look at this!"

The mist drifted across the road, shrouding the woods and pathway ahead with a softness and—I hardly know what word to use—but I'll choose *comfort*.

I had experienced a mist like this before as I hiked along a slope of Whitetop Mountain in Virginia. Then, too, a cloud of vapor had moved through the trees and changed the world around me. As it had then, this mist on a slope in the Pyrenees affected me in ways I find hard to explain.

For one thing, this indefinable entity drifted gently over the landscape and eased the hard, unyielding lines. Details were obscured in its haze, creating a sense of calm and peace. When it disappeared through the forest, I felt a loss. I preferred the pathway shrouded by the mist.

Why did this touch me so? I have yet to work out that answer.

Is the mist like people who pass through our lives, easing the starkness of day-to-day trials with their kindness and gentleness?

Could it answer a longing I sometimes have to clear my mind of the countless minutiae that clamor for my attention and energy? I seek for times that I can blot these out and unclog my senses so that beauty and peace can come through.

Is the mist like the Holy Spirit, who moves through each scene in my life and, while I'm dealing with "reality" He reminds me of the mystery of a reality beyond what my eyes can see? Awareness of that reality can make daily frustrations and hardships lose their sharp edges.

Or does the quiet, gentle mist moving ahead of me bring comfort and gladness because it is a reminder of the cloud that always went ahead of God's people on their journey, and it now reassures me of His presence and guidance?

I'm not sure of the answer. Perhaps all of those thoughts come into play.

I do know this—the mist coming through the beeches was a thing of beauty given to me on this first day of pilgrimage.

4

Ancient Roncesvalles

My first impression of Roncesvalles was that everything is old. So very old. Of course, I knew this. Yet it still amazed me. The ancient buildings and narrow streets in almost every town and village we passed through have been there for hundreds and hundreds of years.

We arrived at the hostel much later than most pilgrims. A new building with 180 beds was already full, so after our passports were stamped, we were directed to an old stone building. This was the original albergue, dating back to the twelfth century and holding an additional 110 beds. This was fine with me. I preferred the historic, traditional hostel.

From the outside, it reminded me of a long barn. Then we stepped inside, and I experienced something of a shock. Imagine, if you can, vaulted ceilings supported by stone arches. High overhead a few windows are cut deep into the unadorned stone walls. Underfoot, a bare stone floor. One can just visualize being in this stone hall in medieval times. But this was 2014 and now—did I mention 110 beds? All in one room. Bunk beds, just a few feet from each other. My first night on the Camino, I'd be sleeping here in this huge dormitory room with a horde of strangers. From my stays in shelters along the Appalachian Trail, I was well acquainted with all of the various nighttime sounds that would soon rise from those bunks. I dreaded the concert of many voices that was sure to flow toward the vaulted ceiling that night.

At this large albergue, we were assigned a bed number. In some hostels, pilgrims simply pick out a bunk from whatever is available, and groups coming in early are encouraged to take the upper bunks and leave the lower ones for latecomers. Here, with 290 beds, I'm sure they needed the organization of assigned bunks to prevent chaos.

We went in search of our beds, and it soon became apparent that older folks were assigned to the lower bunks. Life was easier in a lower bunk. If you were in the upper, when you climbed up to your mattress to retire for the night, you also wanted to be certain you had everything you'd need— water bottle, headphones, cell phone, and any other paraphernalia of personal accessories required. Otherwise, if there was a need for an item during the night, down you climb. Then up again.

My gray-hair advantage lasted only a few days. Lori soon noticed that I could scamper up and down those ladders just as quickly as a twenty-year-old. (My hiking and biking journeys had developed agile legs.) She eventually insisted I take my turn in the upper bunks.

Walking down the long rows of beds stacked two high, I observed clothes hanging at every possible spot and backpacks lying on the floor. This hostel was nothing like what I had known on the Appalachian Trail. Everything felt far removed from my world of comfort. I was lonely and, admittedly, a bit scared, even though we were surrounded by humanity. Snippets of conversations in unfamiliar languages drifted to my ears; it's a strange sensation to find oneself surrounded by words, none of which you understand. My sense of being out of place was growing into apprehension. With many languages bouncing off the stone walls and much bustling about in the small spaces between beds, I imagined myself at the site of the tower of Babel.

Finding my assigned bunk, I stared in consternation.

"There are no blankets! Or pillows!" I exclaimed.

Lori looked at me. My disquiet must have been obvious.

"That's why you brought your sleeping bag."

Oh. I had forgotten. Yes, I had packed a sleeping bag.

We settled our possessions and I headed down to the lower level of the building for a shower.

Many folks who are considering doing the Camino hike soon find in their research that privacy is not at all what we in the United States consider *privacy*. You may have guessed at that already, with only one room and 110 beds for both men and women. Showers and bathrooms are also often shared.

Everyone uses the same showers and toilet stalls. Not at the same time, of course. But don't expect to find doors labeled *Ladies* or *Gentlemen* in all hostels.

Could some embarrassing situations occur? Of course. I had no experiences of uncomfortable encounters such as this, but then, I wasn't looking for such things. I was on *el Camino de Santiago* for reasons other than that.

If you are considering the pilgrimage and are concerned about this, you can be sure that the Camino grapevine will give you information about accommodations in hostels. For example, we heard of one albergue where the shower stalls did not have doors or curtains. We avoided that and stayed elsewhere.

Many other lodging options exist in towns along the way and you can find private rooms—in hotels, inns, and even homes. In some towns, you'll find upscale Paradors, a chain of luxurious hotels, many of which are historic buildings that have been modernized. Private lodging is a choice, but you will not have the entire experience of the Camino if you miss the albergues. (The albergues are hostels reserved for pilgrims. Many other hostels also cater to tourists and other travelers, in addition to pilgrims. We occasionally chose hostels that were not designated albergues.)

I sought out and found the showers—and, much to my dismay, they were also sadly lacking. Lacking towels. Where are the towels?

Back upstairs I went to inquire. Someone informed me that pilgrims are expected to bring their own. Hmm. I must have missed that point in my research at home.

"But," the man replied, trying to be helpful, "there's often one or two lying around somewhere."

So back downstairs I went, on a hunt for a towel left and perhaps forgotten by some other pilgrim. None presented itself, but in a small laundry area I did find an abandoned pillowcase. That could work.

It did.

After my shower, the pillowcase was returned to the spot where I had found it, and I went upstairs to join Lori and Aoife for supper.

The *credencial del peregrino*—my pilgrim's passport—also entitled me to a pilgrim's meal, usually at special prices in restaurants, cafés, and bars along the Camino. Lori, Aoife, and I went to a nearby restaurant. It was very busy, but we found a table for three.

The waiter approached and, without even asking, placed a bottle of wine on the table. At many restaurants, the pilgrim meal is simply brought and set down in front of you—no menu decisions required. This waiter must have thought we knew what we were doing. Some places would ask us what we'd like, but menu choices are considerably higher in cost. Pilgrim meals always consisted of three courses: soup; a main course, often chicken or fish and vegetables; and dessert. Dessert was usually ice cream or flan, a type of custard. The meal was always accompanied by a bottle of local wine.

The chicken noodle soup was delicious, and I ate three bowlfuls. Then came the chicken—I thought. It was very dark and not very good, but I ate it. After I'd finished, one of the ladies told me it was duck. My first experience with a pilgrim meal was also my first taste of duck.

We had come into town so late that I'd had no chance to explore my surroundings, so I took a walk after supper. Our hostel was part of a large monastery complex. At one time, a hospital here at the monastery cared for pilgrims who had suffered injury or disease as they came across the Pyrenees. A small Gothic church, no longer in use, is called the Chapel of the Pilgrims, or the Chapel of Santiago, or the Chapel of Saint James. A bell hanging in its tower was once used in a chapel on the mountain; the monks rang it to guide pilgrims through the mountain mists.

Adjacent to the chapel is a long, lower building called the Silo of Charlemagne. The two buildings together represented exactly what I would find all along the Camino—statues and memorials from a history that spans thousands of years and, interwoven with that, the stories and traditions of faith, specifically many events associated with *Santiago,* or St. James.

The Silo of Charlemagne, also called the Chapel of the Holy Spirit, is supposedly built over the burial place of the same Roland whose name we had seen on the fountain just before we crossed the cattle border guard into Spain. Sir Roland was one of the best knights of Charlemagne, the emperor of France about 1200 years ago, who tried to unite all of Western Europe under his rule. The Moors had crossed the Strait of Gibraltar and conquered Spain and were moving steadily northward. On one campaign, Roland and Charlemagne marched the French army into Spain to stop the Moors, and their route took them across the Pyrenees through many areas we pilgrims also walked through. Charlemagne had promised that these towns in Navarra of Spain—Basque territory—would not be harmed as he and his army traveled through, but on their return to France, they did not honor that pledge. In revenge, the Navarrese Basques attacked and destroyed the rear guard of the army. Supposedly, the bodies of many of those knights and nobles, including Roland himself, were buried here. Many years later, the building called the Silo of Charlemagne or the Chapel of the Holy Spirit was built over the burial spot. Throughout the town and the entire mountainous area, there are monuments and memorials that recall the time of Charlemagne and Roland.

As nearly as historians can agree, pilgrimages to Santiago (at the other end of northwestern Spain) began almost two centuries after that Battle of Roncesvalles. The town is located in a pass through the mountains, hence Charlemagne's choice of route and also the pilgrims' use of this path. In the twelfth century, this Benedictine monastery in which we were staying was built, and it soon became a refuge and respite for pilgrims. Over the years, pilgrims on the Camino who died at the monastery hospital or on the nearby trail were also interred in the chapel called the Silo of Charlemagne.

The tiny chapel right next door, called the Chapel of the Pilgrims or the Chapel of Saint James, stands as a testimonial to a thousand years of spiritual significance of the Way of Saint James.

Who was this James who became the patron saint of Spain?

When Jesus picked his twelve apostles from among a greater number of followers, two of the men had the same name. James, son of Zebedee, became known as James "The Greater" to distinguish him from James "The Lessor," the son Of Alphaeus. (Some think that was simply because he was taller than James the Lessor.) To further confuse facts, Jesus had a brother named James who became a leader in the early Jerusalem church and authored the book of James in the New Testament. James the Greater, son of Zebedee, disciple of Jesus, brother of John, is the character I'll be following on the Way.

The official ending of the Camino de Santiago at the cathedral in Santiago de Compostela is where the supposed bones or "relics" of the Apostle James lie.

How they got there is an amazing story. It may be just a story, or perhaps with enough imagination, suspension of belief, and a dab of faith (make that a lot of faith), it just could have, might have, perhaps have—well, there is a possibility it did happen as I'll explain it.

5

Disciples

There are many variations to this story, so let just preface it by saying this is my version, a blending of numerous narratives.

The story begins back in the year AD 30, as Jesus started his public teaching. It's interesting to me that Jesus always walked, too. At least, the Gospels never mention Him riding anything at all until the week before His arrest and crucifixion, when He borrowed a donkey for a ride into Jerusalem. Perhaps His walking can be attributed simply to His culture and economic status, but I like to think that His hiking tours of the countryside offered Him the perfect settings and opportunities to teach His followers.

Imagine a day beside the Sea of Galilee. Jesus was strolling along the shoreline with a crowd following Him. He was teaching, but at the same time, He kept His eyes open for folks He wanted to ask to join Him. He was preparing to put His team together for the work ahead of Him.

There were many groups of religious people from which He could have chosen.

The Zealots advocated an armed revolt against the government. But Jesus was teaching peace, so He probably saw little chance of finding candidates from that group who would dedicate themselves to His vision.

The Sadducees lived only for today and didn't believe in life after death, although they liked to appear as pious people. They sat on the high court or council that ruled Jewish life but still tried to appease the Roman governors. Almost everything Jesus was teaching went against their status quo. It would have been foolish for a Sadducee to give serious consideration to becoming a follower. They were much more interested in trapping Jesus in debates on religious points and thus discrediting Him.

The mainstream religious party of the day, the Pharisees, were diligently attempting to follow all dictates of the law regarding Sabbath observance, feast days, and a multitude of rules and regulations regarding cleanliness. Jesus, though, was planning to lift that burden from mankind.

One group might have shown promise of representation—the Essenes. They were pacifist in nature, and that certainly would have fit with Jesus' teachings. However, they were also hard to find. They removed themselves from society, forming cult-like groups and living in caves out in the desert. The Essenes also attempted to follow the law in all its trivialities, even refusing their body the luxury of pooping on the Sabbath. Well, excuse my French (at least until I hit Spain on this trail), but that is just ridiculous in my opinion. I can imagine those poor folks sequestered in their stone house, squirming miserably, watching the sun with anticipation—because sundown would signal the end of the Sabbath and herald an acceptable time for what would have been a much-needed potty break.

That really didn't leave Jesus much choice but to scrounge about for followers—most of the time, outside the religious establishment. In the end, He chose folks much like you and I.

Or did He?

Back to our lakeside scene.

On that particular day, two fisherman brothers were working with their nets by the shore, and in these men Jesus saw potential. Calling out to them, He offered a proposition.

"How about leaving those nets and joining me in fishing for people?"

The Gospels don't record any hesitation or debate or even going home to throw a few things in backpacks. Simon and Andrew tossed their nets aside and followed Jesus.

That does seem like an impulsive reaction, does it not? Did they think their partners would retrieve the nets? Were they also tossing their jobs and livelihood? What did their wives think about this disruption of their family life and income source?

Soon after, Jesus saw two of their partners, James and his younger brother John, out in a boat with their father, Zebedee. Before Simon or Andrew could say a word about the abandoned nets that someone really should stow away, Jesus had called out a similar invitation to these two brothers.

"How about you two? Are you interested?"

Whatever your impression may be of these four fishermen, they certainly could make snap decisions. I can see James and John leaping overboard and splashing their way to shore, leaving bewildered Zebedee to manhandle the nets solo. I wonder what Salome, Mrs. Zebedee, thought that evening at the supper table when Zeb informed her that her sons had abandoned the family business. Or perhaps this family had already heard about what Jesus was teaching and were waiting for an invitation to join Him, then jumped when He did give them the opportunity. We do read that Salome also became a supporter of Jesus' ministry. Not sure what happened to Zebedee though.

James, John, and Peter became Jesus' confidants. We don't know the reasons, but Jesus seemed to be closer to these three than to the rest of His disciples. They were with Jesus throughout most of His three years in the public eye and were witness to things the other disciples had no knowledge of. Some historians believe that Salome was Mary's sister, and thus James and John and Jesus were cousins. If that's true, then Jesus would have grown up with them and they possibly knew a great deal about Him before He came walking along that day.

Jesus' friendship with these three is interesting. Look at their characters. Zebedee's two sons were rather impetuous and forthright, perhaps even with a bit of a temper problem.

Jesus took to calling the brothers *Boanerges* which meant *sons of thunder*. They even had the audacity to ask Jesus for ringside seats next to Him when He set up His kingdom. And then there was Peter. In spite of all Peter's rough edges, Jesus must have seen the potential in him. Peter was brash, outspoken, and more likely to leap before he looked, yet he and Jesus shared a strong bond. Scriptures say Jesus chose His circle of twelve "to be with Him." And for whatever reasons, Jesus kept these three especially close.

So this James, son of Zebedee, probably knew the human Jesus better than anyone other than John and Peter. James was there after the resurrection when Jesus met His disciples on a mountain in Galilee and told them that He had been given all authority in Heaven and on earth, and they were now to go to all the nations and make more disciples.

Even then, some of the disciples questioned what was happening. Can you imagine the scene? Eleven of Jesus' closest associates, looking at a man they had seen executed. Now He's standing in front of them and talking to them—yet they don't know what to make of it all. Some of them doubted. I wonder if Thomas was still among the doubters. I doubt it.

James had seen and heard so much during Jesus' ministry that he certainly was not among the doubters and must have believed every word His teacher spoke. He believed he had been commissioned to go out himself as a teacher and disciple-maker. He believed he was to go to the ends of the earth on this mission, and he believed Jesus would be with him wherever he went.

So he went.

Through various travels, James ended up in Galicia, the northwest province of Spain, at the edge of the Atlantic and what was then known as the edge of the earth, and he preached there for a number of years. When he returned to Jerusalem at one point, Herod's grandson, also named Herod, was on the throne and quite opposed to the young Christian church. Someone pointed out to Herod a particularly strong leader of the church—our James—and the apostle was arrested and beheaded, the first martyr of the church, about 11 years after Jesus Christ's crucifixion. One tradition says that the person who had betrayed James was so impressed with the steadfastness of James's faith as he received his sentence that he, too, decided to be a Christian, asked forgiveness of the apostle, and both were then beheaded the same day with the same sword. Quite a different ending than the story of Judas's betrayal.

The disciples of James wanted the body to go back to Spain. One version says that some disciples accompanied the body, others claim that it was placed on a stone ship with no crew. Somewhere off the coast of Galicia, a storm sank the boat but the body washed ashore, covered with scallops, which are so common there. Another tradition says that a wedding was taking place close to the shore, and the horse on which the bridegroom was riding was spooked by the sight of the stone ship—and he promptly took himself and his rider into the sea. Miraculously, they emerged alive—covered with the scallops.

The body of James seems to have been lost for hundreds of years. Then a peasant was led by a bright star to a field where he discovered a grave with the bones of several people. After all the proper and official proceedings by the Catholic Church (of which I know nothing, I admit) the remains were pronounced by the Pope to be the bones of St. James and two of his disciples. The bones of James are now interred in a casket in the great cathedral of Santiago. The full name of the city is Santiago de Compostela; *compostela* is thought to come from the Latin *campus,* meaning *field,* and *stellae,* meaning *stars.* The entire name: Saint James of the Field of Stars.

Charlemagne had crossed the Pyrenees to fight the Moors in 778. The story of the field of stars and the discovery of the bones of James came in 813.

But the story of the apostle James does not end with his body miraculously reaching Spain and then being found again by guidance of a star, or with being interred in a magnificent cathedral and having a city named after him. Legend has it that James appeared several times over the next four hundred years as Christians fought the Moors for control of Spain. In battles, St. James appeared at critical times, riding a horse and slaying the enemy, turning the tide of the battle. He became the protector and patron saint of Spain.

Stories sprang up concerning miracles associated with the bones of St. James interred at the cathedral. Folks began to make the trek to Santiago de Compostela to seek miracles they needed for their own lives or to gain forgiveness for their sins. Starting from the doorway of their homes all over Europe, they were fueled by faith as they undertook, via many paths, the pilgrimage to the sacred site where lay the remains of the apostle.

Today, there are other routes originating in other places than St. Jean in France. All converge at the tomb of St. James. Along the way, constant reminders give encouragement in the form of crosses and statues or images of St. James, now depicted as a pilgrim himself. No longer the hot-headed disciple or the sword-wielding protector, in most places he appears as a gentle traveler, with hat and staff and scallop shells attached to his clothing.

This history lesson now brings us to this humble pilgrim in 2014, thousands of years away from *Santiago,* the apostle, and generally unacquainted with him. I would meet him, or his imagined image at least, all along this trail. He had taken seriously Jesus' invitation to follow. I claimed to have also accepted the invitation, but many of the old questions kept popping up and I wondered, *Am I doing this right? What should I be doing as a follower of Jesus Christ? Apostle James went to the end of the earth. Would I do that?*

Here I was, a Mennonite on a Catholic pilgrimage. What would this apostle's life teach me about following Jesus?

My 109 roommates were settling in for the night. Along one end of the building was a long table with dozens of charging units for cell phones. Some pilgrims sat there, guarding their possessions. A few days later we learned that someone had stolen a number of cell phones at a nearby albergue. We quickly learned to be very vigilant about our phones. I was especially so, not because I needed to stay connected but because all my photographs were on my phone.

A cat wandered in the door and led a chase around the huge room, jumping over beds or ducking under the lower bunks. The commotion went on for a while, until the pursuers finally gave up. I never did find out if the cat stayed the night or found its way back outside.

In my bunk, I expected it was going to be a long night so I immediately put on my Bose headphones. Every now and then, I did take it off just to listen to this experience. Although it was unsettling now, this milieu would become my comfort zone over the next six weeks: snoring, snippets of hushed conversations, plastic bags crackling, and other rustling about. Folks from all over the world were gathered here, and most of them knew only one or two other people they were hiking with and, like me, understood almost nothing of the various languages flying about.

Wrapped in my sleeping bag, I thought about the next day. In this hostel alone, 300 pilgrims were lodged. At least one other inn offered accommodations in this town. At this time of the year, statistics say a thousand people a day leave St. Jean, and additional pilgrims come to the Camino at Roncesvalles and begin their walk here. In the morning, 500 to 600 people would be starting out toward Santiago from these streets. Who would I meet? With whom would I make connections? What would my days be like? I felt a little bit of apprehension.

All right, it was a big apprehension.

6

Basque Country

At six o'clock in the morning, an orchestra woke up all pilgrims. Imagine an orchestra playing an energetic melody, the notes resounding throughout a high-ceilinged stone hall. It was recorded music, but it got the job done.

    This second morning we set a pattern we would follow for most of the next four weeks. The small group I hiked with started off early, walked an hour or so, then stopped for breakfast about the time the cafés and bars (as the small restaurants are called) opened for business. When we checked into a hostel, we usually tried to find a bunk close to an exit so that we could easily slip out the next morning without creating too great a disturbance.

Leaving Roncesvalles, we passed the sign I had seen the night before: *Santiago de Compostela 790.* That was 790 kilometers between us and Santiago, about 491 miles. The path immediately began descending. This day would be much easier than the climb over the Pyrenees, although we were still in hilly terrain.

The morning was misty as we walked along a woodland path under the canopy of trees and high shrubbery. At many places, the Camino ran alongside the highway, and we could hear the traffic even though we did not see it. And even though we had started early, there were already other pilgrims on the path ahead of us.

Monster slugs began to appear on our pathway. Seven or eight inches long, their black ugliness was repulsive. Every now and then a mess on the path told the story of one squashed by someone's boot, but I couldn't even imagine doing that—it would feel like stepping on a little rabbit.

We stopped for breakfast at a café in Burguete, a small town that grew up along the Way of Saint James to serve the needs of pilgrims. With white houses under red-tiled roofs in a beautiful green valley, Burguete was a favorite fishing destination for the American author Ernest Hemingway. This town and the city of Pamplona were made famous by his novel *The Sun Also Rises,* set in this same area. This was definitely "Hemingway country." Although I could not always read the language of signs, I recognized the name *Hemingway.* Sites here have become something of a tourist attraction for those wanting to retrace the footsteps of the famous author.

By the time we stopped at a café, dozens of other pilgrims had arrived, and the area was already littered with backpacks.

Although I left my restaurant managing job seven years before, I still enjoy watching whatever is happening at such eateries. I can feel the atmosphere of a place and instinctively sense things that are going on with the staff—things of which customers are often oblivious. As I walked across Spain, I marveled at the contrast of their food service to what we have come to expect and even demand in the United States. During my time in Spain, I saw no sense of urgency whatsoever and very little organization. In food service (at least, in the U.S.), prepping is a huge deal. With 200,000 hikers coming through each year, I would have expected that these cafés and bars would be highly organized and efficient, but it seems as though proprietors are content to make just enough money to support their lives. Many times, we would go up to the counter and could only hope to get the attention of someone and be served. We'd place our order, and *then* prepping and preparing took place. Would you like a glass of juice? The orange will be juiced right then.

Of course, some of the confusion and what appeared to be disorganization must have come from serving folks who were speaking many different languages. My guidebook had warned that most local inhabitants we would meet do not speak English and have no desire to learn it. The guide even gave a list of common phrases we often used and suggested strongly that it would be good if we learned these Spanish words as part of our preparation for the Camino. I had not done so. After all, Lori spoke Spanish well enough for both of us. (But in retrospect, I see that assumption was on the same level as my assumption that she was providing a roof over my head with her three-person tent.)

Nearly all the cafés did have very modern cappuccino makers. At first, I was apprehensive when ordering coffee; I had heard that Europeans drink theirs very strong and I usually prefer mine fairly mild. I learned to order my coffee *Americano,* which is basically a watered-down version. Even so, it was stronger than what I drink at home, but I did learn to enjoy it because it was not bitter.

At noon, we'd often stop at a bar and review their *tapas,* small dishes we would call appetizers or snacks. They'd be lined up on the bar and I simply pointed at what I thought looked good. Sometimes I did ask Lori to translate and tell me what a particular dish was. It gave her an opportunity to rib me about hiking the entire Camino without learning Spanish. Many Spanish words sound much like their equivalent English words, so I wasn't always entirely clueless.

I did learn several words and phrases, though. *Buen Camino* is a frequent exchange between pilgrims and given by locals as we passed by. *Buen* means *good. Buen Camino* is something like wishing someone a good day or good night—except that on the Camino it means *Have a good path, Have a good journey,* or *Good traveling!* We heard this dozens of times a day.

Even when traffic was limited or vehicles were entirely prohibited, we did have to stay alert for two-wheeled traffic. Bicycles are permitted on the Camino. We considered them a nuisance. Sometimes we were walking along in contemplative silence or quiet conversation, and suddenly a group of bikes was upon us. We appreciated those who rang a bell to warn us of their approach, but many times we had no warning. Some businesses along the trail will rent bicycles to folks, and I suppose it is one way to see the Camino in a short time, but again, cyclists lose a major part of the pilgrimage experience. Riding a bicycle gives one no quiet time when the mind is free for reflection; the mind must always stay busy with navigation, alert for obstacles and other traffic. Those atop bicycle seats also have little connection to walking pilgrims. The riders flew by us and we never saw them again. If you're among the riders, you might connect with people in your own group but never anyone else.

One of the first cycling groups to pass us consisted of four young Italian men. They zipped by us, but not so fast that we did not take notice of the biking attire of one. He was wearing shorts. Not Bermudas or biking, but—undershorts. That's it. No shirt. No pants. Just his underwear.

Much more pleasant than watching the cyclists was inhaling the beauty of the flowers. Their cheerful colors greeted us along the path and in every village.

The old stone bridges were amazing in both beauty and engineering. How is it that these ancient spans have endured for hundreds of years, but our highly-technical work disintegrates within one or two generations?

Every now and then along the way, we came upon pilgrim-made markers, sometimes created with the most unusual things like an old shoe or a hat or a stack of rocks. Is this how the medieval pilgrims found their way to Santiago? Did they search for helpful signs left by those who went before them? Most of the time, the yellow arrows are easily followed, but those indicators are a recent addition to the waymarking on the Camino. What did the first pilgrims follow?

I loved following the yellow arrows into the little villages, walking into the midst of daily life that has carried on its traditions for generations. I've known small towns in the U.S. that host thousands of travelers every year, and we capitalists are always tempted to set up all kinds of businesses catering to tourists. Some of our villages have lost the flavor of daily life; now they are simply what we call tourist traps. You'd expect that these Spanish towns would do something similar. With so many travelers passing through, wouldn't they have commercialized the Camino pilgrimage to make a buck or two from the traffic? They have not. Not even the cafés and bars have shifted their focus toward tourism. If you find a small local deli or bar, you stop in for a bite. Every now and then a new albergue was opening and an old one closing, but no one was capitalizing on the traffic of passing pilgrims. I could feel the genuine life in these villages, the deep roots of families going back generations, and it always delighted me.

At two o'clock in the afternoon, everything in town shuts down. It doesn't matter what's going on, two o'clock is siesta time. If we arrived in town sometime between two o'clock and five o'clock, our first impression was often that the town was dead. We would see no one and find almost no business open.

This long afternoon nap is probably necessary because at night when I was trying to sleep, the towns would be very much alive. Chairs and tables are pulled out into the streets in front of houses, and people are laughing and drinking and having a great time. Kids run everywhere, playing and shouting—and I'm trying to sleep. By ten or eleven the children are home in bed, but the adults are often out until the early morning hours. No wonder they set aside three hours of every afternoon as naptime.

On this second day, we walked up and down and up and down. The terrain was no longer mountainous, but sometimes steep grades led us up to a ridge and then down again. Finally we reached Zubiri, an industrial town in a river valley.

My guidebook suggested stopping here. *Don't overextend yourself on these first few days,* the text advised. However, for those with the energy, another option is just 5.5 kilometers (3.5 miles) down the road.

We had the energy, and passed by the medieval bridge that crosses the river and leads into Zubiri and walked on to Larrasoaña.

This tiny town has centuries-old ties with the Way of Saint James. In medieval times, a monastery existed here, along with two hospitals for pilgrims. *Two hospitals?* One wonders what shape pilgrims were in by the time they reached Larrasoaña.

An ancient stone bridge arches over the river and enters the town. This one was called *Puente de los Bandidos*, the bridge of the bandits. Apparently, it was the perfect spot for thugs to ambush pilgrims coming into the village. No wonder they needed two hospitals. Or perhaps pilgrims were easy prey at this point because they were so sick and weak coming in from the trail. Either way, the bandits are now gone. Or so I assumed.

We passed safely and entered the town during siesta time. Perhaps the bandits were simply napping. Everyone else in town certainly was.

When we checked into the hostel, we had a room slightly more private than the 110-bed dorm room in Roncesvalles.

Our room had only five beds, and Aoife, Lori, and I shared it with two Italian men who were very loud and boisterous—the result of a little too much alcohol. They were hiking with a group who was going only to Pamplona, about 20 kilometers down the road.

One of the Italians was named Paul. At supper later in the evening, he realized that my name was also Paul, and so of course we were immediate friends. I had no idea what he was saying, and he had no idea what I was saying, but we communicated somehow, shouting back and forth and waving our arms. Paul (the other one) had more than enough alcohol in his system and so things just got louder and louder. This is typical on the Camino—many languages meet, but somehow folks still communicate even though we're unable to recognize the other's words.

Earlier that evening I had had another lesson in language and communication. We had found a small grocery store offering free wifi. After purchasing something to eat, we sat outside to use their technology. Lori conversed with the proprietor in Spanish but could not comprehend everything he said. We three struggled through a conversation where I attempted to discover where he was from and how he had learned his Spanish which even to my ear was different than the Spanish spoken elsewhere. He had lived in this village all his life, he said, but he was adamant that he was not from Spain. He was Basque. He was not speaking Spanish. He was speaking Basque. The Basque people, I was learning, have a strong, independent identity.

After Basque country would come the second segment of Camino Francés, the flat and hot plateau called the Meseta. I'd read that many hikers quit at the Meseta because they find it boring. Finally, the third and last section of the trail would be Galicia, at the northwest corner of Spain, a farming area with more hills and much rain. I'd had my fill of rainy, muddy trails as I hiked through Maine on the Appalachian Trail, but for some reason I had not packed my rain gear for the Camino walk. Perhaps that had just been wishful thinking.

7

Pamplona

Was it possible, I wondered, that on Day Three of my Camino hike, I might accomplish a goal I had cherished for most of my adult life?

In our sights this day was the city of Pamplona. At one time, just the name of that city would send me into reveries involving intrepid daring on my part.

Pamplona is the city famous for a tradition known as the running of the bulls. Now, many of us young Amish and Mennonite boys have run *from* the bulls in our childhood, but if you're wondering how I came to be dreaming of participating in a strange tradition of a Spanish festival, then read on.

I grew up in a strict Conservative Mennonite tradition, and our house had no spot for a television. So I read books and books and more books. Many of them were boys' adventures like the Hardy boys and Zane Grey westerns. Then, in high school, a teacher piqued my interest in other literature and I became acquainted with those authors someone somewhere at some time has decided to call "great"—writers like Henry David Thoreau (my favorite), John Steinbeck, Edgar Allan Poe, Mark Twain, and many others. Ernest Hemingway became one of my literary heroes; I found his novels fascinating. Much of the world did likewise, when, back in the early twentieth century, they read Hemingway's vivid stories about a small, unknown town in Spain and its yearly "running of the bulls." Suddenly, Pamplona *was* famous as folks started to arrive to both watch and participate in the event.

The running of the bulls is one of the highlights of the festival of San Fermín, a patron saint of the Navarra region through which we were now walking. Fermín lived back in the third century. The son of a Roman stationed in Pamplona, he converted to Christianity and became a priest and later a bishop. But his spreading of the Gospel met fierce resistance, and he was beheaded while preaching in France. The festival, held every year from July 6 to July 14 in Pamplona, honors this martyr.

A much-anticipated event during the festival is the running of the bulls. If you were a farm kid, perhaps you remember bringing the cows home from the pasture into the barn? This is a similar concept. Except that this is much more dangerous. And the beasts being herded through the cobblestone streets aren't placid bovines. They aren't headed for a safe barn, either. The bulls are released from a corral into the narrow streets of Pamplona where they chase runners who lead them through a fenced route of about a half mile. The chase ends at the bullring, where the animals are held in pens until they meet their demise in an evening bullfight.

Often the runners are people who come back year after year to participate. It's dangerous—people have been gored and killed. Many, many have been injured.

And if I, your intrepid author, was ever fortunate enough to be in Pamplona, I did think that I might possibly want a taste of this adventure.

We walked a bit in the morning before stopping for breakfast. An enterprising fellow has built himself an open-air food stand right alongside the Camino. The small brick kitchen area is protected by a tiled roof with three odd chimneys, but there is no dining room. I'd call it a Camino take-out.

We went to the counter and ordered, then stood or sat wherever we could to eat tasty breakfast sandwiches. This restaurant manager was more organized than most. Prep work had been done. Juices stood ready. From the ceiling hung samples of currency he had collected from pilgrims hailing from all over the world. A few steps away was a small albergue; I assumed it was also run by this entrepreneur.

Crossing the River Arga by way of the Puente de Magdalena (Bridge of Magdalena), we walked over the beautiful stone arches that support the walkway known as the pilgrim's entrance to Pamplona. A stone's throw away, automobiles flew by us on the highway, across a very modern bridge. Only a short time before, we had been in an ancient countryside village, now modern city scenes took shape around us. It was something of a shock to the senses. I recalled a similar feeling on the Appalachian Trail when, after several days of hiking through the forest and traveling at 2 miles per hour, we suddenly came to a place where the trail crossed a freeway and cars were whizzing by at 70 miles per hour.

Pamplona was the first of the larger cities we walked through, a very modern town with over 200,000 inhabitants. Tourists find plenty to see and do—museums, shopping, a grand cathedral, historic and religious sites, and many other attractions. As in our own large urban areas in the States, we saw sprawl and industrialization. But in most of these cities, the Camino scallop shell and the yellow arrows bypassed all the other attractions and led us through the centuries-old section of town which was often right in the middle of the city.

Some pilgrims choose to spend time in Pamplona to see the sites. The Italian group we had occasionally met on the trail ended their walk here. I cannot say I was sorry to part ways with them. They were just happy and loud. But if one is on the Camino for solitude and contemplation, even joyful noise is sometimes unwelcome.

Walking over an ancient drawbridge and then through a stone arch, we entered the old, medieval part of Pamplona. As we had seen in so many of the smaller villages, the town was adorned with flowers. No matter how old or crumbling the buildings were, most had colorful, blooming plants on steps and porches and walkways. People who plant flowers have an appreciation of nature's beauty. Perhaps they can even be said to be co-creators with God. I often stopped and sniffed and took in the marvels of floral splendor.

A bread truck was parked in the street, making deliveries. Quite unlike the bread that always arrived at my restaurant, these aromatic baked goods were simply stacked, unwrapped, in open crates. The scene illustrated the intriguing mix of ancient and modern in these cities, where a new city has grown up around a very old one and new ways mix with the old traditions.

Stopping in a bar (café) for lunch, we surveyed the tapas displayed on the countertop. My choices that day were based on easily identifiable ingredients. One was an egg inside a red pepper. I also chose something that was cut into pie-shaped wedges, obviously an egg and potato dish. A few days later, I was told this dish is called a Spanish tortilla. It was delicious. Lori asked about vegetarian dishes. The guidebook warns that vegetarians often have difficulty finding suitable meals on the Camino, but restaurants usually could accommodate Lori's tastes. She often ordered paella, a vegetable and rice dish with rice and more rice. Since chicken or seafood is sometimes added to this dish as a variation, she always inquired if the paella was *con carne*. I soon deduced that this meant "with meat."

More important than the food were the connections we made with other pilgrims at these stops. We greeted others we had seen on the trail and met new faces that we would hike with over the next few days.

At this stop, Grace and Zoe became part of our Camino journey. From Australia, these two were aunt and niece. Zoe had recently lost her mother, Grace's sister. The two were hiking the Camino, hoping the pilgrimage would bring some healing to both. We would walk with them for much of hike.

Another pilgrim in what I called the Aussie contingent was Simon. He was an interesting man. More on Simon and his adventures later.

A girl from Cleveland was on the Camino looking for discernment concerning her future. Would it be more schooling or a job?

And two Scottish ladies, whom I guessed to be several years older than I, were on a yearly adventure together. They'd left their husbands behind (for a short while, at least) and appeared to be having the time of their lives.

Aoife and most of these people we had just met planned to stay in Pamplona that night, but since it was early in the day, Lori and I walked three miles further to Cizur Menor where, we had learned, the setting includes a pleasant courtyard and garden.

The Pamplona suburb of Cizur Menor sits on a promontory and looks out over the surrounding area. That evening, after a pilgrim meal at the restaurant next door, I stood outside the albergue and looked back at Pamplona, considering the fact that I had actually been in the famous city—and had not given a thought to the scenes of my daydreams. The running of the bulls was over for another year (I had missed it by a month), but I would have imagined that if I finally arrived in Pamplona after all those years of dreaming about it, I would have at least sought out the streets, the corral, the bullring, the motel, and all those sites that Hemingway had made so famous.

But I had not.

Perhaps it was no longer important. Isn't it interesting how places or events you dream about and long for lose their luster when you actually arrive? Sometimes, we are only excited about the possibility of someday doing this thing or going to that place. I had been in Pamplona—and walked right through. The dream of intrepid daring was no longer important. I was not on the Camino to be stomped by angry bulls.

Much more important that evening was the death of another dream—the hope that my North Face pants would live forever.

Understand, these sturdy pants have been trustworthy companions on many adventures. I wore them every day for five months on the Appalachian Trail. (Yes, I did wash them occasionally.) Then they served me well every day for two and a half months on the cross-country bike ride. They ventured forth with me yet again as I sailed (staggered) through nine days of misery on the Mississippi River. And I cannot even count the shorter hikes on which they assisted me. Oh, my, what a pair of pants!

But now, only three days into the Camino walk, they had suffered a grievous injury. A four-inch laceration at the knee had me worried.

The proprietor at the hostel was training a young lady on procedures for checking in pilgrims when I approached and showed her the tear.

"Is there any chance you might have some thread to repair this?" She did. She handed me a small sewing kit with thread and a needle.

I tried to look helpless. She didn't take the hint. Or perhaps she did take it but then rejected it.

So I went back to the dorm area and found Lori. Lori, the nurse. Lori, the nurse who surely stitches up injuries every day.

"Lori," I said. "Look. Tear. Needle. Thread."

The nurse took the needle and threaded it carefully. Then she handed it back to me.

"I don't sew," she said.

"But you're a nurse!"

"Yes, I am. I'm a nurse, not a doctor. I don't stitch."

And she was gone.

So I would have to do it myself. I understood the basic concept. You stick the needle in, push it around a bit and jab yourself, then bring it back to the surface.

When I finished, the stitches didn't look too bad. My knee smarted a bit where I had stabbed myself with the needle. Lesson one from Camino Day Three: Take off the pants before stitching.

I did take them off before going to sleep that night and hung them over the foot of the bed.

In the morning, the thread had somehow untangled itself, slithered out of the fabric of the pants, and dropped to the floor. It lay there, taunting me.

I have since been informed of what must be Lesson Two that day: Knot the thread when you've finished stitching.

And from other feedback I've had concerning this situation, I think you have to do something unusual at the beginning, too.

It all added up to one profound insight: Men should never be allowed near a needle and thread.

8
Winds Across the Way

Not far from Pamplona is a ridge of mountains called the Sierra del Perdón, "the mountains of forgiveness." Our path would lead to one particular peak, Alto del Perdón, the height of forgiveness.

As we departed from Cizur Menor and began the morning walk through a farming valley, off to our left we could see the outlines of huge windmills rising from the ridge into the sky. The long row of dozens of turbines produces power for Pamplona. Supposedly, there are days in Spain when wind power alone can return enough power to the grid to supply the entire country. We saw hundreds of the giants on the hilltops as we hiked through the rolling hills.

We started up the steep path toward the ridge, and soon the whooshing of the massive blades beat a rhythm with the whooshing sounds coming from our lungs.

Just before reaching the height of forgiveness, pilgrims often stop at a stone water fountain set in a semicircle of a low stone wall that also serves as a resting place. The spring, however, was dry. It often is. This is the Fuenta Reniega, the fountain of denial or renouncement.

At this spot, legend says, a weary pilgrim arrived, thirsty and near collapse, but the spring he expected to find had run dry. The devil disguised himself as another pilgrim and offered to show the weary traveler a gusher of fresh water—on one condition. The thirsty pilgrim must renounce his faith in God.

It seems that since the beginning of time, the devil has favored this strategy, tempting folks at the point when we are weakest and most vulnerable. If he can, he'll catch us when we are parched—anything to stop us from reaching the pinnacle of forgiveness.

Of course, our pilgrim of legend would not give up his faith. He resisted. And the devil fled. (I don't know if legend includes that fleeing devil or not. I added it, because we're told by Scripture that this will be the result of resistance.) And then St. James himself appeared, produced a spring of refreshing water, and used his own scallop shell to serve the weary pilgrim.

We pushed on to the top of Alto del Perdón. A sculpture there honors Camino pilgrims. The monument consists of a series of life-sized iron silhouettes depicting a string of pilgrims, some walking, some on horseback, headed toward Santiago.

This mountaintop might have the strongest winds on the entire Camino. An inscription reads (in Spanish, of course): "Where the way of the wind crosses the way of the stars." The depiction is perfect in this setting—pilgrims are bent into the wind, their hair and clothes billowing behind them. Most are medieval pilgrims, judging from their dress. But at the very back of the line, two modern figures with backpacks follow the earlier pilgrims.

From the high ridge we could see the small towns ahead of us on the Camino. I loved those glimpses we were given of what lay ahead. I looked forward to each town with anticipation, wondering who resided there, what *life* happened there, and what part of it we would share. As we walked through the streets, past folks in their gardens or visiting with a neighbor, past children playing and clothes waving in the breeze on a clothesline, we passed through scenes from the life of a town that has existed for centuries. We were products of a different culture and another kind of life, but we all gave and received the same greeting many times a day. *Buen Camino.*

We are all pilgrims, walking the same paths that many have walked before us.

In every country and every culture and every age, we share the journey. From the moment we are evicted from our mother's womb, we are on pilgrimage.

Welcome, Pilgrim.

A slap on our bottoms both welcomes us and sends us off to begin our journey to somewhere. If each tiny infant could comprehend the magnitude of the situation, it would be something like this:

Welcome to life, you little sinner. You had no choices up to this point, but from here on out, your life will be filled with crossroads of decision.

On your pilgrimage, little one, the pathway will not always be easy. You will encounter diversions, stumbling blocks, and other impediments that hinder your pilgrimage.

You see, little bundle of potential joy, there is an ending to this journey you are embarking on today. Choose wisely and your pilgrimage could be on a pathway marked Straight and Narrow. Be assured that Straight and Narrow also goes straight down through deep valleys but at other times soars over mountaintops where the view is grand. The good news is that at the end of that pilgrimage, you die. The better news is that you get to live forever in unimagined bliss.

About this time, the little bundle would be thinking, *Sounds great. Quit weighing and measuring me and get some clothes on me. It's freezing out here.*

Furthermore, little bundle of potential trouble, there is also a pathway marked Broad. This wide road may seem appealing at times, but it is quite deceptive. Do not squander your pilgrimage on this road. Broad leads to destruction. Not only destruction of family and relationships, but eternal destruction. Yes, little one, the bad news is you die. The worse news is that you'll live forever in unimagined horror. That's a grim pill, Pilgrim.

Waaaa! Put me back where I came from right now!

Here's the kicker, newly arrived bundle of innocence. The nasty road leading to darkness is your default setting. Oh yes, I know it seems beyond the realm of what we like to call fairness. You who have done nothing wrong to date are doomed—unless you make a conscious choice to change paths.

That, dear reader and fellow pilgrims, is an imaginary conversation none of us had at birth. Nevertheless, it is the harsh reality of being born into this world.

But why must it be that way? Would it not be so much easier to be born into a world where the pathway to eternal bliss is the default setting and Heaven is assured unless one deliberately chooses the way of destruction?

Wouldn't Matthew 7:13 read so much better if it said, "The gate is wide and the road is broad leading to life and many enter there?"

But it reads quite differently, and so we know that finding the narrow gate spoken of in the same chapter will take a deliberate choice.

But how do we find the narrow gate on our pilgrimage through life?

Have you ever wondered why God seemed to make it so difficult to find that gate? What does it really mean to walk the narrow pathway? Is it difficult? Is it even possible?

The Bible speaks of folks who thought they were on the right pathway, yet God greeted them with a dismissal. *Go away, I don't know you.* Now, that is just about the most brutal thing anyone can imagine. You thought you were doing it right, but yet you missed the mark.

These iron pilgrims at the top of Alto del Perdón have their faces set firmly in one direction. They seem pretty certain of their road. The wind batters them constantly, but they are not blown hither and yon. How can we know for sure we are heading in the right direction? How do we chart our course and keep it in spite of punishing winds? Or do we just do the best we can and fumble and bumble along and take our chances? That sure seems like too much of a risk.

9
Lightening Up

The descent down the other side of the mountain was equally steep and probably more dangerous than climbing. The loose gravel made footing unreliable and even I who love downhills had to slow my usual pace.

Leaving the green foothills of the Pyrenees behind, we now were walking a countryside of farmland and vineyards, although the fields looked brown and arid to my eyes.

This day was August 13. One year before on August 13, I was in one of the circles of Mississippi hell (recounted in *Mississippi Misadventure*). And seven years before, I was standing on Mt. Katahdin, celebrating the end of my Appalachian Trail hike, on the 13th of August.

Although I thought that those journeys had thoroughly educated me on the perils of carrying too much weight, I decided on this August 13 that once again, in spite of my good intentions, I had packed in excess.

We do this in life, too. Determined to run the race with lighter loads, we must still be on guard against picking up more weight, letting Satan or our culture or even our friends and family weigh us down with burdens that keep us from running well. Yes, sometimes we ourselves are the culprits, adding to our own heavy load.

On this day, I was thinking about the unnecessary load I carried—I would sort it out and let go of everything I did not need. The pack on my back seemed to get heavier and heavier and reminded me of the pack I had carried every day on the Appalachian Trail.

I did pare down that weight as much as possible. My AT hike might not have survived if I would not have done so. But I refused to slack pack (hike with a lighter day pack). And I climbed the final mountain with the pack on my back, even though most hikers leave theirs at the ranger station for the day's climb. I had a reason for dragging that load along with me.

As I trudged along on the AT, every day I thought about the sign at the summit of Mt. Katahdin. It would signal the end of my long journey, but I also saw that simple wooden sign as a cross, and I imagined myself carrying my bag of garbage and shame up to the cross—where I wanted to drop it. That's why my burden had to go up the mountain with me. I had to dump it. So when I finally reached the sign and I dropped my pack and fell on my knees, I wept with both relief and joy. I was finally letting go of my heavy burden.

On the Camino, I also carried my pack every day. Some hostels offer the service of shuttling backpacks ahead to the next destination so that pilgrims need only carry a light day pack. I did not even consider this. There is something about carrying the necessities of survival with you, on your back, but at the same time choosing wisely what you do carry, so that you can run the race as well as possible.

But today, August 13, I determined it was time to once again lighten my load.

This was also a day to make one more attempt to save my North Face pants.

Walking through an arched stone doorway, we entered the streets of a larger city, Puente la Reina. I was walking the Camino Francés, the route to Santiago de Compostela that begins in St. Jean or Roncesvalles, France. But there are at least a dozen other beginning points and routes in Western Europe, and these Caminos all eventually merge and make their way to Santiago. Here in Puente la Reina, the Camino Francés is joined by one of those routes, and so the number of pilgrims increases. The next day, we would leave the town over a magnificent bridge of six graceful arches. The bridge was built by a queen in the eleventh century, specifically for the use of pilgrims, and it is named the same as the town, the Spanish equivalent of "Bridge of the Queen."

Our accommodations for the night were in a monastery known for its extensive gardens. I love living, growing things and spent some time walking through and admiring the well-kept plots of flowers and vegetables.

The beds in the monastery are distributed throughout twelve rooms with eight beds in each. However, both men and women use the same bathroom facilities. In one long room, commode and shower stalls lined the wall. There are dividers and doors for privacy, but this more relaxed attitude toward privacy does take some getting used to. It's not for everyone. I never did adapt completely to that—nor did I want to. I was always careful to give others privacy and desired it for myself, too.

In the shower rooms, a line of sinks also offers pilgrims the option of hand washing their clothes. Most hostels have a place to hang clothes to dry, a line strung up somewhere in a courtyard. Clothes dry quickly in the hot winds. At this hostel, there is a small area with washing machines available for pilgrims to use, but the line of backpacks waiting to dump their contents into a washer was long and sometimes spots were contested. It was easier to simply wear my shirt into the shower and wash it as I lathered up. Then I'd rinse it out and hang it and my towel out to dry.

My daily household chores included once again seeking help for the laceration in my pants. I asked at the front desk for needle and thread. Thinking I had surely gained some expertise from my first attempt at stitching, I sat down in the dining room to try again. But apparently I looked hopeless and confused. A lady I had never met before offered to sew it up for me, and I gladly handed over the tools and my pants. Yes, I had already changed into another pair.

Into the old, narrow streets we went, in search of supper. Aoife was with us once again. After staying the night in Pamplona, she had caught up with us that day. We chose a little café on a cobblestone street lined with shops and eateries. Our table was set outside, but every once in a while, a car came along and we'd have to get up and pull back the table and chairs so that the car had room to pass.

Since Lori and I had both determined to shed some of the weight in our backpacks, I took time that evening to assess everything I was carrying. My guidebook would have to stay. Sure, most of the time I hiked with other people and many carried this same book, but always borrowing the book or asking for information would be both impractical and inconsiderate. But there was another book, one I had brought along to read. I'd finished it already on the flight over the Atlantic. I carried an iPad and an iPhone. I suppose I could have survived with only the phone, but …

It happens all too easily, this being weighed down with unnecessary things.

In the end, I shaved 5 pounds off my load. That may not sound like a lot to you, sitting there in a chair and reading these words. But when those extra 5 pounds rest on your shoulders, kilometer after kilometer, up the mountains and down steep slopes, then every ounce is felt. My AT pack had weighed 35 pounds; now I was carrying 22, but even so, my shoulders were hurting. Every unnecessary ounce would have to go.

Our normal routine of walking in the early morning before breakfast was abandoned the next day because we had to wait for the post office to open so we could mail our extra weight home. The 5 pounds I wanted to ship to the States would have cost me between $80 and $100, so Lori and I collaborated on Plan B. For a much more reasonable flat rate, we could pack a box about 18 inches square, ship it ahead to Santiago, and pick it up once we arrived there. We both stuffed our unwanted pounds into one box and sent it off.

Our walk started late that day, but as we crossed the bridge of six arches that had weathered a thousand years of pilgrim feet, it felt wonderful to be rid of the extra weight.

10
New Faces

The many windmills on the hills in this part of Spain reminded me of Don Quixote and Merele Kinsey. If you know either of these gentlemen, you might be wondering at my association of these two. Allow me to explain.

Mr. Kinsey was the literature teacher who had introduced me to writers that opened up my imagination and had me running with the bulls. Sometime in one of my literature classes I had heard the phrase *tilting at windmills.* Although I confess that my mind was often roaming around outdoors while my body sat indoors, that phrase did catch my attention and stuck with me. When the words popped up again later in my adult life, I decided it was time to read the book that gave rise to this expression. Strangely, the English saying came from a Spanish novel, *The Ingenious Gentleman Don Quixote of La Mancha*, written in the early 1600s. The book has remained a classic through the last three centuries. Our gentleman Don Quixote was an idealist who set out on adventures to restore chivalry to Spain. One day, he mistook windmills for enemy giants, and he drew his sword to engage them. His sidekick had to bring him back to reality, but the phrase "tilting at windmills" has been part of our language ever since, used to describe someone who is on the offensive against an imagined enemy.

I never would have known about Don Quixote or his skewed view of reality were it not for Merele Kinsey. One teacher planted seeds of love for literature that sprouted and grew—have been growing, as a matter of fact, for all of my life. But he had no idea of his influence until just recently.

When I published my first novel, I decided to dedicate it to the teachers who had had an impact on my life so long ago. I did my research, wondering who was still among the land of the living. Yes, it *was* long ago, and many had already passed, Merele Kinsey among them. I regretted never thanking any of these teachers for their contributions to my life. Teachers are often unappreciated; even more often they are not *told* of our appreciation. And it's not only teachers who do not receive our thanks—there are many people who have enriched our lives and made a difference in our destinies. Have we acknowledged their gift to us?

After the book had been released, imagine my shock when I opened my email one day to find a message from Merele Kinsey. *Ah*, I thought, *Heaven has internet!* It turned out that my research had found the obituary of another man by the same name. My old Lit teacher was still alive and well. We've since met several times, and when I explained how his influence had affected my life, he responded with, "I never knew if I made a difference."

I've been thinking about all the people who have crossed my path in life and helped to shape my pilgrimage. Many of them I have yet to thank. In some cases, it's too late for me to express my gratitude. I regret that.

Remember to thank other pilgrims who have helped you along your path.

We were walking through rolling hills of farm country with an increasing number of vineyards. In the fields at times we saw huge stacks of hay—not haystacks as we know them, piled up loosely and somewhat rounded, but neat, rectangular stacks made up of bales stacked twelve high and as many as thirty bales long and a dozen wide. From a distance, these hay stacks almost looked like buildings in the fields.

As the road wound through the countryside ahead of us, we would sometimes look ahead and see a small town crowning a gentle hill. I loved those scenes. No suburbs, no sprawl. Perhaps a cemetery and a vineyard on the slopes outside the town. These towns have been there for at least a thousand years, with all their traditions and deep roots of generations of families. True, many of the young folks feel compelled to seek employment elsewhere in Europe, and thus the towns often seem filled only with old folks and young children, but the life there always intrigued me. I'd see the town ahead and feel the mystery of life within its old buildings that crowded narrow, twisting streets.

Almost always, the towns were adorned with flowers. Recessed windows in the stone buildings created deep window sills that were often filled with green plants or blossoming flora, and balconies on the second or third floors were lined with pots filled with blooms. The unusual and distinctive doors on many homes also made the walk through town a joy. Front entrances were of many varied colors and bedecked with all sorts of items. Apparently when these houses are remodeled, the family keeps the door and uses it again. Some are so uniquely designed or decorated that they are works of art, and many of these doors made me wonder about the stories of the family within.

In one of those small towns, we heard someone call to us as we walked along. Simon, the Australian we had met back in Pamplona, was sitting in front of a little grocery store that looked nothing like a grocery store, but more like a house. Simon, assured us there was food to be had inside, and not wanting to miss this opportunity for nourishment, we investigated. We brought our purchases outside and sat and chatted with Simon as we ate.

Again, several new faces joined our journey. A German husband and wife were on vacation and hiking the Camino. He was an officer in the German army. She was a flirt. To my mind, they seemed a very strange couple. In their mid-twenties, they hiked apart, perhaps because the husband didn't seem to know what to do with his wife and her behavior. It seemed the only way she had of interacting with men was to make eyes at them and tease and toy with them. She loved the game of leading on any man whose attention she could capture. Her husband acted just as strangely; he simply chuckled and went along with her outrageous behavior.

The Flirt had already captured one luckless chap. Her prey was a young man who had walked several thousand kilometers, all the way from his home in Holland. Nick was a sad and lonely looking fellow. According to him, he had been walking for months and had made no friendships at all along the way.

When Nick met The Flirt, he fell in love. I cannot tell you what he was thinking. The woman was married, after all. I have even less of a guess at what she was thinking. But I do know what I would have thought if I had been her husband ...

But I digress. Back to our story.

Nick's first real connection (the Flirt does not count as a real connection) came that day. He and Simon developed a friendship. Simon was in his early fifties, a retired coal miner. While he was traveling the world, he was also in the process of selling his home in Australia and buying a small ranch out in the country where he wanted to develop something like a bed and breakfast. I enjoyed Simon. He was an intelligent person who knew a lot about a lot, and he always had an entertaining story or two waiting to be told.

Nick, on the other hand, did not know what he wanted to do with his life. He was in his early twenties, from a family of engineers, and was broke. His current plan seemed to be to simply keep walking, as long as there was a road ahead of him. He had no purpose in doing so. It was just that he didn't know what else to do. He ran out of money and wired home for more.

At first, his parents had sent him funds; then, after frequent requests for more money, they told Nick they'd buy him a ticket home but would send no more money. So he was living pretty much by mooching off other pilgrims or sympathetic locals.

Simon seemed to like Nick and enjoyed his company. That could have been because they had one thing in common: They both loved to drink. Simon was willing to buy the drinks and Nick was willing to drink them.

Here I also met Maria, a university student from the Czech Republic. She would play a part in Act III of the Saga of the Great North Face Pants when, the next evening, the slice in my pants was again opening up and she industriously took up needle and thread (she knew what she was doing) and stitched up the wound once again.

We had planned to stay in the main albergue at Estella, but it was already full when we arrived.

Many Americans hiking the Camino use the same guidebook I had, *A Pilgrim's Guide to the Camino de Santiago* by John Brierley. The author has hiked the Camino many times, and he gives suggested starting and stopping points for each day, with his choice of albergue at each day's destination. As a result, the town he has indicated as a stopping point for the day is bombarded with people. It doesn't take long before you start thinking that if you don't get up early and you don't keep up the pace for the day, you'll get to town later than everyone else and there might be no room available. Many people do worry about this. In the morning, there's a rush to get on the road and get to the next town.

If you find yourself on the Camino, do not, I repeat, do not, let yourself be caught in this mentality. In the first place, when your pilgrimage has become a rush to get from one place to another just to secure a room, then you are no longer on pilgrimage. You have lost whatever it is that you've come to the Camino for. In the second place, there are many other lodging accommodations beside the suggested hostel. There will be another town and another albergue or hostel or inn. In some towns, you'll even find the luxury of upscale hotels. Brierley's suggestions are helpful and practical, but his choices are not your only options. You'll be able to find a room somewhere.

We did not get a room at Estella's main albergue, but we had other choices. We decided on a hostel across an old bridge and up a hill. This was run by a German priest and well known by the German pilgrim community. I especially enjoyed communicating in German that evening.

This hostel in Estella was also the site of my blessing another pilgrim. Never mind the fact that my deed was unintentional. I'm sure it made someone happy.

You'll remember that in Roncesvalles on that first bewildering and overwhelming night, I borrowed a pillowcase to dry off after my shower. Two days later, while walking through Pamplona, I passed a fabric shop and stopped in, buying a long piece of fluffy cotton that I intended to use as a towel.

That evening in Cizur Menor, I realized the towel was the size of a beach towel, took up too much space in my backpack, and added too much weight. So I cut the fabric in half and left one part at the albergue, hoping to make someone's day.

Two nights later I made another hiker's day when I accidentally left my towel in the shower room in Estella.

Thus, I was once again towel-less. But pilgrimage does teach you to make do. A tee shirt served quite nicely for the duration of the hike.

11

Black-Sheep Follower

If you've been along with me on any of my other adventures, you know I consider tradition to be a necessary part of the full experience of a place. There was Naked Hiker Day on the Appalachian Trail. And that half-gallon of ice cream I ate at one sitting.

But one Camino tradition was becoming most annoying. My clattering scallop shell put my forbearance to the test. I was on the verge of tossing tradition.

The scallop shell has become the symbol the Camino. Back in the early days of the pilgrimage, travelers would pick up shells on the Galician coast and carry them back home as proof that they had indeed walked all the way to the end of the earth. Then the shell's utilitarian qualities were noticed: it could be used as a dipper for water or even a scoop for food. At the outset of the hike, pilgrims now take shells and attach them to their packs or clothing or tie them around the neck as a symbol of the journey they're undertaking.

Mine was attached to my pack in such a way that the shell often rattled as I walked. The clattering was tolerable for a while but soon became as aggravating as a dripping faucet. Then I'd resort to a shrug or two of the shoulders or dancing a few steps to shift my load and quiet the chattering thing.

This morning, my chatty companion would not be shushed.

Another tradition on the Camino is a stop at the Bodegas Irache, a winery in this vineyard country. In one wall of that winery, a fountain dispenses free wine to travelers, who drink it from their scallop shells. I knew the fountain was ahead of us, and I remarked to Lori that perhaps a bit of wine would silence my shell.

"Oh, yes, and that works so well for you, too, doesn't it?" she retorted.

She had noticed that even a small amount of wine had the effect of making me more talkative.

In my growing up years, anything of an alcoholic nature was denied admittance to the Stutzman household. Here in Europe, though, a glass of wine is customarily included with meals, and I did partake of that. Sure, there are those pilgrims who indulge to excess. I did not. I'm a quiet person by nature, and I like to control what comes out from within. But I too had felt the connection between my brain and my tongue loosened just a bit by the glass of wine served with meals.

She may have also been referring to my occasional attempts at conversation on the trail when she was not inclined to talk. I like intelligent exchanges and light banter, and there were times I wanted to indulge in a bit of badinage, but Lori just wanted to cry. Grieving, at those moments she was no more in the mood for profound or entertaining words from me than I was for that clatter and chatter of the scallop shell.

Acres of vineyards lined our path as we walked that morning. When we came to the winery, we stopped for a few sips of wine from our scallop shells. It was no surprise to see Nick show up for the free drinks. The Flirt was also there, as was her husband. Most pilgrims make a stop at this fountain. It's tradition.

We took a detour that day. All right, we were lost. Briefly. Although even that is not quite accurate. Never actually "lost," we could at times see the road we wanted to be on and pilgrims walking along on it—it's just that we weren't on that road. We'd taken a wrong turn.

At the intersection of two roads, the yellow arrows, which were usually so clear and unambiguous, seemed to point in two different ways. Two arrows on two different sides of an old farm building forced us to make a choice. One arrow pointed straight ahead, leading us onto a narrow dirt road. The other would have sent us around a curve and toward the highway.

We went straight ahead. Eventually that dirt road curved, too, toward the highway, and by then we realized there were no more waymarks, no signs or arrows encouraging us onward. Across the highway, we could see people walking along another path while we were walking on what seemed like a farm lane through a field.

An extra mile or two was added to our hike that day, but perhaps our wrong turn was because I needed to see the flock of sheep in that lane.

They were headed toward us, a flowing tide of woolly creatures, completely filling the lane and raising a cloud of dust as they trotted along. Before we met head on, they turned into a side lane and veered off to our left. We watched as dozens, perhaps a hundred, of them followed the shepherd who walked out in front of the flock. At the very end came a few stragglers, including the proverbial black sheep.

The scene reminded me of Jesus' words comparing Himself to the shepherd who leads His flock. During the few minutes that it took for the sea of wool to pass, I wondered where I was in that flock. Was I at the front, with my nose right at the heels of the Shepherd? Was I somewhere in the middle?

I knew where I was. I was the black sheep, coming along at the edge of the crowd, lingering on the fringes of the flock.

My spiritual questions once more came to the surface. That black sheep represented where I felt I was spiritually—at the edge of the traditional church, out there on the fringes of the life of the flock.

Just as our energies and our mental acuity move through various cycles of vitality and faintness—in other words, we have our ups and downs—so too our spiritual lives go through these fluctuations. In the period of time that I made a practice of reading my Bible through twice a year, I was one of the sheep trotting along right up there at the heels of the

Shepherd, following closely, wanting to hear everything He said. I heard His words daily, and they changed my life. Then I finished my AT hike and began a new career focused on writing, and I didn't dig into the Word as much as I had before. That changed my life too. I felt I was lagging behind, a little further away from the Shepherd than I had been.

This was the root of the questions that kept bubbling up. Was I following Jesus in this life I now have? I thought so. But was I doing it right? Should I be doing something more? Should I be shouldering my way up there toward the front? I was hanging around the fringes, sometimes a little more adventurous than those in the middle of the flock, sometimes doing things a little differently than what was expected. Yes, I was still a part of the flock, and I still knew my Shepherd's voice, and I'm certain if I got lost He would come find me and bring me back. But *should* I be doing something more, something different?

Was it okay to be back here, dawdling along on the fringes?

James the apostle was present when Jesus charged His disciples with going into all the world to make more disciples. James took the mission seriously. He had gone to what was then the end of the earth. But I wonder—did he ever have questions like the ones that swirled around in my head? Did he ever wonder exactly *where* he was supposed to go? Did he ever wonder if he had understood correctly, if he was doing it right? Did he ever examine his days and ask, *Should I be doing more?*

Part of my answer came that very day as I pondered the black sheep on the fringes and thought about how my life has changed over the past few years.

When I set off on my AT hike, I was planning to write a book after I returned home. The best-seller would be about my adventure and my wise and profound reflections on life in general. But during the hike, God spoke to me and gave me another message to include in my book. I was not especially enamored with what He told me to write. I protested.

I'm not the one for the job. That's a job for preachers.

No, God insisted. This assignment was for me. I would write a book and touch lives that preachers and churches would never reach.

How's that gonna happen? A fair question, really, since I had never written a book before and I believed I was too much of a cracked pot for God to use.

God would make it happen. That was the promise. He'd get the book into the hands of folks who needed to read it.

And He did. The book was published, and many things came about in ways that "just don't happen" in the publishing world. God was in charge of sales, and I started getting letters and emails from all corners of the country and from folks in all sorts of situations. God is still touching people's lives through that book. I'm still in awe. When I read an email from someone who "just happened" to pick up the book and "just happened" to find in its pages exactly what they needed to hear at the time, I wonder how all of this came about. The answer can only be that God's purpose used my obedience.

Now I myself needed a touch, a word, a reassurance. The question that has chased me all my life was still hounding me: Am I doing enough to deserve God's favor?

The answer, of course, is no, I am not.

None of us could ever do enough to deserve all God has done and is doing for us. We can't earn God's favor. Our relationship to Him does not depend on what we do *for Him*. Instead, everything depends on what Christ did *for us*. That's a difficult idea to grasp when you have been conditioned to think of *being saved* and *following Jesus* as a long list of Thou Shalts and an even longer list of Thou Shalt Nots. It is not a matter of what we do, it is a matter of who we trust.

James the fisherman must have trusted Jesus completely. He did not hesitate one moment before jumping out of his old life and into a new, unknown one. I had done the same thing. When I tell the story of my AT hike, I talk about the huge risk I took, leaving a good job when it made no sense at all. But looking back now, thinking about Jesus' calling of His disciples, perhaps I was only looking at the "risk" through the world's eyes. Perhaps, when you *know* who is calling you, following Him is not such a big risk after all.

If we decide to be a Christ follower, then we are also signing on as partners in His mission in this world. God has instilled in each of us skills and abilities He can use in the mission. He places us in situations where He wants us to make use of those skills.

James understood that. Some versions of his story claim that his attempts to evangelize Spain were pretty much a failure, but he was obedient to the commission given him. And even if the historical fact really was that he did not see fruit of his preaching, the seeds were sown. Here on this Camino de Santiago, I was witnessing the harvest of seeds planted centuries ago.

I've signed on to follow Christ. I've been sent on the same mission as James. I do have questions sometimes, but I'm still listening to the Shepherd's voice and following Him.

That day, on a dusty road I never intended to take, God gave me one answer. He has led me to the place I now walk. Assurance came that my assignment for now is on the fringes. When I was up there walking so closely to the Shepherd, my soul was fed constantly, but I never turned around and touched other lives. Now, living on the fringes, I am feeding others and keeping them company as we all trot along, following our Shepherd.

12

Choice

Los Arcos was bursting with festivities when we arrived. Were they expecting us? Banners flapped in the wind. A band played. Down the street came a procession of people, some carrying small statues on platforms—I assumed they represented a saint. Nearly everyone was dressed entirely in white with red scarves knotted around their necks or red sashes flowing from waists.

We had walked into another celebration of the festival of San Fermín. Held in July in Pamplona, the festival is celebrated at other times in many other towns throughout Navarra.

Our hostel faced the main street of Los Arcos, at an intersection just off the town square. When we checked in, we were told immediately we'd have to get out. Not necessarily at that same moment, but we did need to leave the building by two o'clock that afternoon because the albergue would be locked up. The running of the bulls would be held in the street right outside.

Here I was, finally, a witness to this famous spectacle!

I watched the preparations with interest. Wooden fences were set up to block off the streets and to put a barricade between bulls and spectators. At the arena, I watched the bulls being unloaded. The beasts looked fairly calm. *Not much more than cows with horns*, I thought.

Back at the albergue, the building was locked, as we'd been warned. A crowd was assembling behind the barricades along the streets, and above us, an old grandmother leaned on the railing of her balcony, watching and waiting. I found a spot beside an elderly couple standing against the wall. The man had on a white shirt and red scarf, and he kept yelling the same words over and over. I had no idea what he was saying, but I don't think his shouts were directed at me.

Hooves clattered on the cobblestone street. Some of the men running ahead of the bulls wore the white clothes and red scarves, but there were also pilgrims who climbed the fence and dropped into the street to join the madness. An official list of rules prohibits running while drunk or drugged, but I do believe that alcohol plays a big part in the bravado of pilgrims who impulsively enter the stampede.

There was no alcohol in my system, but my foot rested on the bottom plank of the wooden fence and my body tensed, ready to climb over the barricade.

Now's your chance. You've always dreamed about this. Get in there and do it.

My body was ready. My mind paused and considered.

You know, it will be harder to stay right here, on this side of the fence than to jump into the street.

It would have been so easy to go over that fence and stand in front of those bulls—that is, until I started running like crazy.

It would have been easy. It really wasn't much of a stampede. The animals did not look like crazed, bloodthirsty killers. They were trotting along, not charging madly. Sometimes one would stop and look around, as though he were enjoying the attention. And the street offered plenty of protection. Pillars supporting roofs over walkways were large enough that a man could easily dodge behind one for shelter if a bull got too close. Yes, it would have been easy to run with the bulls for a short fifteen seconds of glory.

But it would be much harder to stay right where I was.

In the few seconds that my body waited while my mind considered, I knew that if I climbed the fence, I would be doing it only to be able to finally say, "Look what I did. I ran with the bulls!" I'd be doing it only so I could write an exciting narrative right now for you, a narrative that would make you wish you'd be lucky enough to be on an adventure in Spain and running with Paul and the bulls instead of sitting in an office or driving a truck or making pizzas. I'd be doing it only so that you would be dazzled by my daring.

Now I'm getting carried away with my own adulation. But isn't that what the world looks for today? Don't people crave affirmation and admiration from others? We all want to know that our life has importance. It seems to me that Facebook and all these selfies that float around feed that compulsion people have to say, "Look at me! Look what I'm doing! Isn't my life amazing?"

When I suspended the Mississippi River trip, some folks saw it as failing to accomplish what I set out to do. I know that. And in a sense, I did fail. Yet I was happy with my choice that day—I chose family rather than being able to say, "I kayaked the entire Mississippi River."

My choice was much more difficult on the Appalachian Trail. I was terribly homesick, and my grandson Isaac was born during my absence. I agonized over that for days. I did have opportunities to go home, but I knew that if I left then, I would never get back to the trail. At that time, the hike was the most important thing in my life. Not that my family meant less to me, but I believe that hike was God-ordained, a trial of fire I had to go through to heal, to establish a new relationship with God, and to launch a new life. It had to be done, no matter how strong the desire was to go home. Perhaps the loneliness and separation from family was a necessary part of the purifying fire.

The Mississippi River adventure was of my own choosing. I'm not certain that idea was born from God's suggestion. After all, He did spit me out of the river and sent a bus to pick me up and hustle me back home to write an important book.

My foot rested on the lower plank of the barricade... and stayed there. Running with the bulls has lost all the allure that it carried for years. I was on a spiritual journey, not a quest to get stomped by a bull. I'm quite at peace with reporting to you that I passed up the opportunity for that adventure.

I'd much rather be running with the fringe of the flock.

Many of the hikers we had met in the last few days showed up in Los Arcos. After the bulls were gone from the streets, the barricades were folded up and put away, and the crowd began to drift away. I wandered through the town center and met Nick, sitting alone on a bench with a beer in hand and looking quite downcast.

"Nick, what's the matter?" I asked as I sat down beside him.

He poured out his forlorn story. He had proposed marriage to The Flirt and she had turned him down.

Well, I thought, *what did he expect? She's already married.*

But Nick, poor soul, had evidently expected a happier outcome.

13

A Healthy Kind of Nuts

Someone must have stolen my shoes during the night. I could not find them on the rack, but I also could not believe that someone would actually steal a pilgrim's shoes. That's like stealing the tires off a car.

Shoes are a very personal item, and mine, especially, make a long-distance hike possible. Many folks suffered from miserable blisters, but my shoes kept my feet blister-free. We had heard scattered reports of shoes being stolen, or I suppose sometimes a pilgrim could pick up the wrong pair of shoes by mistake, like putting on the wrong overcoat after church on a snowy day. But I found it hard to understand why anyone would steal another person's shoes.

Most albergues have a shoe rack in the entryway. They also have a basket or some sort of container where they prefer that pilgrims stash their hiking sticks. I cringed every time I was separated from my rod and staff. Many hikers simply find a stick and bond with that; I had my expensive Leikis. I always worried about those poles hobnobbing with the cheap tree sticks overnight.

But what had happened to my shoes? How does one go on without their shoes? I felt panic rising within.

Upon closer inspection, I found the shoes still on the rack. They were unrecognizable—the layer of dust they had collected the day before had changed their color.

The grapes were purple and ripe. Hanging so close to the path that a pilgrim could reach out and touch them, they beckoned walkers to sample their sweetness. Jesus' disciples picked grain from the fields as they walked, and so I, in good conscience, took the offering of the vineyards.

After one particularly steep climb and descent, the terrain began to flatten out as we headed to Logroño, the capital of the La Rioja region, an area known for its wines. The mountains and hills were behind us as we walked country roads through olive groves and vineyards.

I like to think that Jesus walked for many of the reasons I do. I imagine that as He was walking, He was talking to God, dialoguing with His Father. There's something about ambulating. You aren't operating a car or a bicycle; your mind is free to think while you walk. The physical exertion sends more blood to your brain and a strange thing happens. Your mind rests and at the same time is nourished and invigorated and begins to process things that you've tried to ignore and shove down in the dark nooks and crannies of your brain. That might be why many people are afraid to think—they're fearful of what will finally surface when they allow their brain to actually work.

In case you haven't noticed, the pilgrimage of the Camino de Santiago is not so much about an adventure that happens *to you* as it is about what happens *inside you*, to your mind and heart. (So if you were hoping to find scenes when my life was hanging by a thread, I'll tell you now that you won't find them in the remaining pages.)

You, my friend, may never walk the Camino or the Appalachian Trail. But wherever you are, you can get out and walk. Find a park somewhere. Or a trail. Get away from Facebook and social media. Walk away from all the things that keep your mind so busy every minute of the day. Let your brain rest and let it think. You might find it does its finest work while you're walking.

Many folks do sections of the Camino each year, coming back again and again. Some hikers were walking their second or third complete pilgrimage. I even met one man doing his twelfth hike. He seemed a quiet fellow, but once he was engaged in conversation, he proved to be a wealth of information. He acknowledged he was probably "nuts" to hike this path repeatedly. "But it's a healthy and happy kind of nuts!" he would say cheerfully.

These folks were good sources of information about the albergues in towns ahead of us. Most towns have a municipal hostel, which is usually the largest. Then there are often smaller hostels available. The really desirable spots are claimed early in the afternoon.

We knew where we wanted to stay in the larger city of Logroño. Hiking past industrialized areas and warehouses, hearing all the noise of a large and busy urban area, I felt an assault on my senses after the quiet of the countryside. The scallop shells and arrows are always more difficult to find and follow in the city, and my mind, that had been at rest, was quite agitated as we found our way to the Iglesia de Santiago, a Catholic church on the outskirts of the city. Attached to the church was a small, 15-bed hostel. This was a desired stop for hikers—following the evening mass, the pilgrims fortunate enough to have snagged a bed here were also served a communal meal.

I had my own reason for desiring to stay at this church.

14

Together on the Path

In midafternoon we checked in, settled into our room, and did laundry in the sinks, hanging our clothes out to dry. Lori and I also wandered to the busy town square and had a meal, but my Mennonite mind was focused on the upcoming evening mass.

I was remembering a beautiful Sunday morning deep in the Maine woods. Padre and I were rustling about, breaking camp and getting ready for another day of trudging through mud, muck, and mire.

Padre is a Catholic priest I met on the trail. Like me, he was also attempting a thru-hike. We became good friends—a Mennonite and a Catholic. At one time in my life, that would have seemed impossible, even ludicrous. That was before I knew anyone who belonged to the Catholic Church or knew anything at all about the traditions and beliefs of said faith.

So Padre and I had many discussions about both—traditions and beliefs. I learned about the Pascal mystery, relics, and different natures of sin. That's right. For Catholics, there are mortal sins and venial sins, and a checklist is available to see which sins one has committed. I had a similar checklist in my Conservative Mennonite upbringing. That list outlined everything prohibited in life: movies, TV, ball games, anything with potential for enjoyment (in my opinion). Going to church three times a week, though, was not frowned upon, so three times a week, yours truly was there.

The eye-opener was that Padre and I hold beliefs that are much the same. Imagine my shock. I thought Catholics were... well, way off base. Even more shocking was the realization that Mennonites are just as steeped in and shackled by their traditions as Catholics.

God had a lot to teach me as I trudged from Georgia to Maine. I think He often must have had a good chuckle.

That morning, instead of hoisting his backpack, Padre pulled out a small box that resembled nothing I'd ever seen in the hiking world.

"What do you have there?" the apostle inquired of the padre.

"A portable communion kit," he replied. "I'm celebrating the Eucharist this morning."

My Catholic trail education had already informed me that *Eucharist* equals *communion* in my world. The *Host* is the bread or wafer used when celebrating the Holy Eucharist. This is indeed a very sacred sacrament in the Catholic Church, as it should be in all churches.

My own experience with communion, sadly, did not carry that sacredness. True, it was a somber and reflective time; we were always strongly advised to assess our spiritual condition before partaking. But the spiritual impact was lost on me. I was too obsessed with a detail of the ritual.

In my youth, our church observed communion twice a year. The preacher pinched off a piece of bread from a loaf and handed it to each parishioner. Then the cup was passed to each member, and everyone took a sip. From the same cup! Fortunately, because I was left-handed, I could take the cup and naturally turn it so the clean side came to my lips. At least, I hoped that no other left-hander had sipped before me and the rim was still clean. Sadly, my personal fastidiousness was repulsed by this act that should have been so sacred.

At my friend's reply, communion out in the Maine woods at once seemed like a very special thing, and I wanted a part of it. But I was to learn how sacred the Eucharist was to Padre.

"Can I join you?" I asked my good friend.

I was baffled and stunned by his reply.

"No, you can't."

Padre explained that I could not take communion with him because I did not believe in transubstantiation. That was a long word not in my vocabulary. Catholics believe the bread and wine turn into the body and blood of Jesus when they celebrate the Eucharist. And because I did not believe that, I would not be permitted to partake.

I slunk back a bit and watched as Padre remembered my Lord's death and resurrection. I was an unbeliever, a heathen.

I believed the bread and the wine (well, okay, grape juice in our church) represents and commemorates Christ's broken body and His blood shed for me. I did not believe these symbols actually became body and blood.

I did not argue with Padre that day, but you know me—my stubbornness and persistence. I could not see the reasoning behind this prohibition. I believed in the suffering of Christ, in His atonement for my sins. Why should I be denied sharing in these sacred moments? I determined that sometime, somewhere, I would find a Catholic church that would allow me to join them in celebrating the Eucharist. I confess, though, that my determination might not have been fueled by a desire for a sacred experience, but rather by my propensity for being downright perverse at times, especially when I'm convinced I'm right.

I mentioned the incident to a Catholic friend in New Hampshire. An unusual thing was happening after *Hiking Through* came out—I was hearing from many Catholic folks. Again, God was probably chuckling as He brought these fellow pilgrims across my path to teach me more. My new friend in the Granite State had felt compelled to purchase the book, and although he had left his faith and the Church, he was brought back to faith when he read it. That's a miracle that even I wouldn't dare take credit for. He has started a men's ministry and witnesses to other men in his parish.

He invited me to do a program at a Catholic school in his area and a program at his church. Thus, I found myself at his church one evening, and following the program we were driving back to his home and discussing Catholic and Mennonite beliefs. As I reflected on how many things we have in common, I thought this man might be just the person to right a wrong I had suffered in the Maine woods one Sunday morning.

"You won't believe this, but I was with Padre on the trail one Sunday, and he wouldn't allow me to partake of communion with him."

I was expecting a bit of sympathy. Instead, I heard, "Of course not; he couldn't allow that."

"Oh yes, I know, transubstantiation," I said, half-dejectedly. "How can you believe that? How can you believe the wafer turns into the actual body of Christ and the wine into His blood?"

My friend pointed a finger at me and gave me the most powerful one-word sermon I've ever heard.

"Faith."

That was all he said, just *Faith*.

I was momentarily stunned.

Everything I believe, the foundations of my Christianity—creation, the virgin birth, the death and resurrection of Christ, the Holy Spirit, forgiveness of sins, eternal life—*everything* I believe is predicated on faith.

I pointed my finger back in his direction and simply said, "Man, I've got nothing to say to that. My belief system also hinges on faith."

However, I also knew that some Catholic churches were more liberal and might allow a Mennonite heathen unbeliever to partake of communion. This Camino I was on was a very Catholic hike, with cathedrals dotting the countryside, their towers and spires and crosses often rising against the sky, high above the towns. Surely I could find one church that would allow me to partake.

That's a long explanation of why I was looking forward to the evening mass. Hiking through these old towns, sleeping in centuries-old monasteries, one begins to feel that you're walking in another time and another world. I was shedding the things that lay claim to and rule my days back home, and I felt a clearing of my mind and an opening of my soul.

Perhaps it was not only my perversity that was seeking out a mass to accept me. Perhaps I did need those sacred moments of communion.

My hopes rose when Lori and I walked into the cathedral and found that an American pilgrim was wanted to give a reading as part of the service. She was chosen. No one asked if she was Catholic; she was a Mormon! If a Mormon could be a part of the program, perhaps a Mennonite would also be accepted at the communion table?

The priest spoke in Spanish; a translator communicated his words in English. And in English, perfectly clear and understandable to my ears, the announcement was made that only practicing Catholics were invited to partake.

I considered going up anyway. Yes, I did. No one would know that I was a practicing Mennonite and not a practicing Catholic.

Those thoughts passed quickly. I stayed in my seat. It would have been too disrespectful to sneak up there under false pretenses. Disrespectful to my friends, disrespectful to the Church, and disrespectful to the One whose body was broken and blood was shed to give me a new life.

There was a special blessing for pilgrims, though, and I received that with a clear conscience.

And I determined that if I ever attended a mass where those prohibitive words were not voiced, I would consider it my green light to celebrate the Eucharist.

The common meals in the old monasteries are something special. Pilgrims know it, and there's rarely an empty bed at those hostels.

This evening was also special because it was our last with Aoife. Her holiday was over and she would be leaving the Camino the next morning.

After the mass, pilgrims found their way to an upstairs room for the meal. We could only converse with a few other English-speaking folks, but the spirit of camaraderie on the Camino does not require understood words. Volunteers helped out with the meal, and I learned that an Asian girl sitting across from me had been hiking but had an injury that took her off the trail. She had chosen to stay here and help out in whatever way she could. The priest spoke (in Spanish, of course) and we sang songs. The words were on the wall (in Spanish, of course), and folks tried to join in, whether or not they understood what they were singing.

This was what I was noticing: everyone is on the same path and we all help each other out. Like the woman who sewed up my pants the second time. I did not know her name or speak her language. Yet, like the Good Samaritan, she took the time to bind up a wound. The Camino brings together people from many different walks of life, of different nationalities and cultures, yet they all have the same goal and help each other along the way.

Shouldn't our pilgrimage to our heavenly home be the same?

15

Taking up my Cross

It had been a long, hot 19 miles. When we had left the city of Logroño in the morning, we walked briefly through parks and along a reservoir. Then the trees became sparse, and we found little shade and fewer fountains. My feet were aching as we trudged into Nájera and looked for a motel. For a week, I had pushed my body to the limit, and it was time to lay down the cross of sharing a hostel with snoring people and waiting in line for showers and laundry. I wanted the comfort and privacy of a motel room.

All day I had been thinking about the cross I carried. That morning we had climbed la Grajera, and at its peak had fantastic views back over the city and across the Rioja vineyard country.

At the peak is where I was also reminded to take up my cross as a follower of Jesus.

For a stretch on the ridge of the mountain, a metal fence separated our path from the highway. One pilgrim at some distant time had stopped there at the peak, picked up a few wood chips from a pile nearby, and fashioned a cross, weaving it into the mesh of the fence. Over time, other pilgrims have followed that first example, and now the fence is covered with crosses made of small pieces of wood or bark.

Crosses mark the way of the Camino. A cross has marked out our way to God, too. The crosses are constant reminders of the pilgrimage we're on.

Jesus said that those who want to follow Him must pick up their cross. Daily.

Pick up my cross? The cross is an instrument of torture and death. Picking up my cross and carrying it along on this journey means I'm headed to—and acquiescing to—my death. How's that for an invitation from Jesus? *Come, join me. Let's walk together down this road—straight to your death.*

Was my cross going to be one of those little twig crosses? Or one of those concrete ones I'd seen elsewhere? If I had a choice, I'd take the twig cross, thank you.

Not very long after Jesus uttered the words about His followers picking up their crosses, He was approached by three different people. Each expressed their desire to become a disciple. To each of them, He talked about the life a disciple would lead: no home and, from the sound of things, not even a backpack with an extra set of clothes and rain gear; cut off from the daily relationships of family and friends, even at the most profound times of life like burying family members; and the absolute finality of giving up the life they knew—they could not look back and wish for what they'd left behind.

I read all that and thought *That's a pretty tall order.* Those are things we all want and long for when we don't have them—home, family, the comfort of the known and familiar. Yet Jesus says we have to give them up if we want to follow Him.

Is it possible? Does it mean we have to walk away from family? But doesn't the Bible also say that he who does not care for his own family is worse than an infidel?

What could Jesus have meant when He said we have to give up our lives and die if we want to follow Him and live?

Could it be that I have to be willing to allow everything about my old self to die? Could Jesus be saying that I must leave behind the old life that was centered on *me*, and take on a new life centered on *Him*? Do I have to let go of my old dreams and desires and habits and lifestyle?

Yes, if any of those things conflict with Jesus' teachings. Anything that does not line up with Jesus' teaching has to shrivel up and die and can no longer be a part of this new life of following Jesus.

When I was on the Appalachian Trail, I knew the saying: If hiking this trail beginning to end is not the most important thing in your life, you'll never finish it. I gave up a lot of things that are intrinsically good, and it hurt, it was agonizing—but the one thing I had to do was finish that hike.

If following Jesus is not the most important thing in our lives, we are not going to carry our crosses very long. As soon as something else calls or the going gets tough or painful, we're going to chuck off that cross and bolt away toward our own path.

There was the rich young man who wanted to know how to get to Heaven. He knew all the commandments and had followed them precisely. Yet he felt there was something more he needed to do.

"Yes," Jesus said. "There is one more thing. Give away all your possessions to the poor and come follow me."

That was too tall an order for the young man. His money and possessions were the most important thing in his life. He had centered his life around his wealth. He could not give it up, not even for Jesus and Heaven. He backed down and went away.

It wasn't that his wealth was an evil thing. No, the problem was that his wealth was more important to him than following Jesus.

How many of us are willing to give up what we want when we want it? On a daily basis, are we willing to give up those things that Jesus says need to go if we want to follow Him along His path?

I look at my own life and think, *Well, I'm not sure I can even measure up to that rich man who had followed all the commandments.* Letting go of our own desires and dreams—whether they are good or bad—is torture and death.

The cross stands at intervals along our pilgrimage path and asks each one to reflect: Is following Jesus the most important thing in my life?

Nick had seen his dreams die. Not because he had a choice, though. We met him sitting outside a café with the German couple, but he informed me that The Flirt was no longer speaking with him. Not a word. As a matter of fact, she was being quite mean to him. Poor guy.

It was a long hot day for everyone. In Nájera, Lori and I decided to take a break from trail life. Every so often, it's good to recharge. We had supper with other pilgrims in the town square, but then found accommodations at a motel for the night. Other pilgrims did the same.

Indulging in the luxury, I soaked in the bathtub without having to think about someone else waiting outside the door for their turn. I slept without my Bose headphones; there was no choir of snorers.

But something was missing here in my solitude. *Strange. When I'm in a room with thirty other people, I wish for the quiet and seclusion of a private room. But now I've got it and something's not quite right.*

Yes, the snoring, the flatulence, all the annoyances and noises had become part of my comfort zone—and I actually missed it all.

16

Church Chickens

The motel in Nájera had stamped my passport even though the establishment was not the official Camino albergue. Many towns have municipal hostels, motels, hotels, inns, and guesthouses that are part of the Camino network and are approved to stamp a pilgrim's *credencial.*

It wouldn't have mattered if I had missed a stamp. Nothing would have bothered me the morning we left Nájera. My body was refreshed, and my mind, now released from strain and free to rest, took the opportunity to flat-line.

During the first week on the trail, all sorts of thoughts and contemplations had churned about in my head. On this day, though, every deliberation cleared out of my mind. The brain waves lay low, gently lapping at the shore, barely rippling the surface. Stress was gone. My body moved on autopilot, since no orders were coming from the command center. If there was anything in my head, it was just nothingness. Medically, I might have been brain dead.

Walking along in contemplative silence, I moved in a trance. Other hikers kept pace in front of and behind me and Lori was nearby as was the Australian contingent, but none were part of my world. The only sounds were the crunching of shoes on gravel and the clinking of poles keeping cadence with our steps.

Oh, a few wispy thoughts of home and friends might have drifted through my head. Nothing was invited in to sit awhile and chat, though. And anything of an aggressive or hostile nature was barred completely.

The day was again hot and dry. Green vineyards interspersed with brown fields already harvested created a patchwork on the gentle hills. More and more sunflower fields appeared. At another huge stack of hay bales by the side of the road, an enterprising fellow had set up a table and was selling food and water. Pilgrims rested in the shade of the haystack.

We were also seeing more of the rock cairns, simple and sometimes artistic piles of stones that bore the unspoken message, *I was here.* Many had slips of paper wedged between the rocks, bearing prayers for guidance or words in memory of someone. At places, dozens of these stone towers rose from the dirt, creating a surreal landscape.

At breakfast in the small and ancient town of Azofra, I was eating a cardboard sandwich consisting of an omelet and ham pressed between—did I say cardboard? It was more like plywood. And I was having a little trouble finding the ham. Spain is known for great cheeses and hams. The cheese was always delicious, but the ham was tough, almost like jerky, and sliced so thin it had only one side.

Much to my surprise, Bob and Kristen walked into the café. I had met them the very first day on the trail over the Pyrenees when I had noticed Kristen carrying both her father's backpack and her own. I never expected to see them after that first day, thinking that Bob's back problems would quickly derail their hike. But they were still on the trail and had now caught up with me.

I asked Bob how he was doing. Good, he said. He was feeling pretty strong. For my part, it was wonderful to talk with someone in my native language, with no wild gesticulating required.

Our planned destination that day was Abadía Cistercienses, the albergue in Santo Domingo de la Calzada. Run by Cistercian nuns, it is a hostel with 33 beds divided among 5 sections. The main hostel in town has 210 beds in 10 rooms. Do the math. Although the main hostel is supposedly one of the most modern and comfortable on the trail, we chose the relative peace of the nunnery, and I especially looked forward to hearing vespers sung that evening.

As I neared Santo Domingo, my mind at rest was alert enough to seize on a photo op. A monument to St. James, which looked like a sheet of metal with a silhouette cut out, towered over me. It was twice my size, and I struck a pose standing in the middle of the space cut out to represent the apostle. Stepping over one of his feet, I felt the metal snag my left pant leg—the one still whole—and saw a new, neat slice open up the fabric.

After checking in at our hostel in the old part of the city, we went downtown, bought food, and brought it back to the courtyard to eat at tables set outside and covered with colorful tablecloths. The profusion of flowers made the courtyard a pleasant spot.

Touring the cathedral, I was surprised to see chickens in a cage. Yes, inside the church, in a cage built into the wall. Church chickens, they were.

The town is named for St. Dominic, who lived in the eleventh century. A peasant by birth, he aspired to be a priest, but had done so poorly in his early studies that the monastery turned him away. Still, determined to devote his life to a godly cause, he took to building roads, a bridge, and a hospital for pilgrims coming through the area on their way to Santiago.

Stories abound concerning miracles surrounding the man. One story tells of him building a road through the forest, cutting down trees with only his sickle. When he grew tired and rested, angels took up the sickle and continued his work.

The story of the chickens, memorialized by live chickens in his cathedral to this very day, is thus:

A mother, father, and son were on pilgrimage to Santiago. They stopped at an inn for sustenance, and since the son happened to be quite handsome, the innkeeper's daughter was smitten by the lad.

He had his heart set on pilgrimage, though, and rebuffed her advances. She did not react kindly to rejection and, taking a cue from Joseph of Bible fame, hid a silver goblet in the young man's backpack. She reported it stolen and the sheriff soon apprehended the innocent lad who was immediately strung up from the gallows.

The sheriff, having meted out justice, returned home to enjoy a chicken dinner.

The parents sadly began on their way, but were stopped when they heard their son's voice telling them he was still alive. St. Dominic was holding him up, standing under his feet. (As usual, there are many versions to the story. Some say that the parents even went on to Santiago and on their return trip found their son hanging from the tree but still alive. That makes an unbelievable story even more unbelievable.)

The parents rushed off to the sheriff's house to plead for their son. He had just sat down to his chicken dinner and was not delighted to see company arriving at mealtime, especially this company.

"Santo Domingo has intervened and our son is alive!"

The sheriff shouted that their son was no more alive than the chickens on his table which he was about to devour.

The words were no more than out of his mouth when the cock stood up and crowed loudly, and both rooster and hen grew feathers and flapped around the room.

Of course, how could one argue with that display? The sheriff removed the lad from the gallows and gave him a complete pardon.

The cathedral in Santo Domingo de la Calzada (Saint Dominic of the Road) contains the tomb of this saint. It also contains an elaborate, Gothic chicken coop where a rooster and hen are kept. I toured the church and paid homage to the chickens residing there. Although I might scoff at the story and place it back in the day when people were "ignorant" enough to believe it, it has made me reflect on faith that can believe in the impossible and unbelievable—a faith that we need.

Perhaps some American churches might consider installing chicken coops in their own facilities.

Supper that evening was in the town center with other pilgrims including the Aussies, Simon, Grace, and Zoe. Those three were staying at the Parador, a former hospital that is now an upscale hotel.

That night I dug into my fanny pack where I kept all my valuables and took out the sewing kit I had been given. Sitting on my bunk and with the aid of my headlamp, I attempted to stitch the new slash in my left pant leg. Why it never occurred to me to purchase new pants is still a mystery.

This episode also ended in failure. Instead of neatly closing the slash with my stitches, I finished my work only to hold it up and find that I had sewed the injured fabric to the bottom of my pant leg.

Some things are just too difficult for us mortal men.

17

Doors

The sunflowers were starting to die. At the start of my hike, the sturdy blooms had been robust and full. Now, their leaves were beginning to wrinkle, looking dry and thirsty, and the heavy heads were drooping.

Many of the sunflower fields edged the road just as the vineyards did, and I had noticed that some of the seeds had fallen out. Every now and then I'd see a pattern in the empty spaces on the sunflower face—I could see eyes and a mouth and sometimes a nose peering out at me from the rows. Intrigued by the way nature seemed to be creating some humorous art, I remarked on it to Lori one day.

She gave me a look, one of those I-can't-believe-you'd-actually-think-that kind of look. And in a second I realized the truth.

There was no coincidental dropping of seeds. Passing pilgrims had intentionally plucked out spaces on the large round heads to create the faces that grinned at me as I passed.

Sunflower fields alternated with onion fields and those gave way to harvested wheat fields, all lying under a hot sun. For some time, our path ran parallel to a busy highway. On this day, our tenth, we left the La Rioja region and entered Castile, another area that, like the Basque region, seeks to be independent from Madrid. Like Basque, they also have their own form of Spanish. (Much as we have our regional dialects of Pennsylvania Dutch.) In Castile we would walk the high, arid plateau of the Meseta, the central plains between the mountainous regions of Spain. Some folks leave the Camino here, finding that walking day after day across the flat landscape under hot sun with fewer people and even fewer trees is just too boring. But for a true pilgrim, it's a necessary part of the pilgrimage.

One of the first towns in Castile was the tiny village (population less than 100) of Viloria de la Rioja. This was supposedly the birthplace of St. Dominic, he of road-building and chicken-raising fame.

We were headed to Belorado, a 14.2-mile hike that turned out to be a 14.2-mile bake.

The Australians, who had stayed at the Parador in Santo Domingo the night before, caught up with us, and we hiked with them most of the day. Zoe and Lori were about the same age and had quickly bonded, perhaps because they each found in the other a heart that understood their grief. I suppose that Grace, Zoe's aunt, was something of a mother figure for Lori.

We all enjoyed Simon. He was an incredibly intelligent man. His original intent had been to hike only to León and then take a train north to explore some other areas of Spain, but he had met these fellow Aussies and found a drinking buddy in Nick, and I was beginning to suspect that he would stay on the trail all the way to Santiago. I enjoyed listening to his stories, told in that Australian accent. Adventurous and a man of wide experiences, he reminded me of a real-life Crocodile Dundee. He loved Frank Sinatra, and so he and I sang a repertoire of Sinatra songs as we hiked along.

Did I mention the day was hot? As we approached Belorado, a man in a pickup handed out bottles of cold water with the name of his albergue stamped on the bottle. What a pleasant surprise for a thirsty pilgrim. And what a great marketing tool. It's even in line with something Jesus said about giving a cup of cold water.

The town came into view, set against a backdrop of limestone cliffs. In those cliffs, dark areas looked like windows and doors. Sure enough, these are cave dwellings where hermits at one time found seclusion apart from the rest of society.

Needless to say, we chose the hostel belonging to the man who had greeted us with cold water on the trail. When we checked into the Cuatro Cantones, we ordered supper from a restaurant on site. A patio area and a small swimming pool behind the building created a pleasant place to relax.

First, though, Lori and I headed to the town square for a lunch of fruit and cheese.

After we returned, I strolled around the grounds and then settled myself at one of the patio tables. Kristen appeared and sat down next to me.

"How's your dad doing?" I asked, remembering Bob's back problems.

They had checked in and Bob had immediately gone to his bunk for a nap. He was whipped, Kristen said. And suffering from blisters on his feet. She, too, complained that her feet were hurting. There was something else, though, that was wearing her down even more than the physical strain.

"We argue all the time. We fight about everything. I'm just so tired of it." Two generations, butting heads over every issue or decision. How well we all know that scene. She was on the verge of quitting, I could hear that.

"Kristen," I said, "what you're doing now with your dad is something special. Not the arguing, but this Camino walk. You might not be able to see it now because it's tough, it's a struggle just to get through each day, but sometime when you no longer have your dad, you'll look back and realize that this was a precious time you were given with him."

She listened. I'm not sure she agreed with me, but she did seem to give consideration to my words.

My dispensing of wisdom was suddenly suspended when I realized I did not have my iPad with me. Normally, I was very careful to keep my electronics and other valuables in my sight and possession. But now I did not have my iPad. Where did I leave it?

I went into the hostel, and found Bob sitting on his bunk, awake.

"I can't find my iPad." I began rummaging through my things as panic started to rise within. "It's gone."

"Where did you last have it?" Bob was a sensible man.

I thought. I had last seen it when I slipped it under my leg. Yes, that was it.

When Lori and I were having lunch in the town square, I had slid the iPad between myself and the chair. And then, I must have gotten up and walked away without a thought for what I was leaving behind.

I ran the few blocks back to the outdoor café where we had eaten. Fortunately, it was siesta time and the streets were deserted. There on my chair, waiting for me, was the iPad.

That evening at our communal meal, a new face appeared. A tall Japanese man we had never seen before sat at the same table as Lori and I. We did not converse; I assumed he could not speak English. After the meal, he quietly disappeared. He would reappear again, later on the trail, always carrying a guitar which we never heard him play—but he would remain a mystery man to Santiago and beyond.

The Camino de Santiago takes one on a journey through an intriguing mural of both national and religious historic fact and beloved legend. The stucco and stone buildings that have baked in the sun for hundreds of years, the amazing architecture of churches and cathedrals, and the ubiquitous monuments to heroes and saints are all infused with many generations of faith, fact, and folklore.

Daily life, founded on centuries-old tradition that is now tinged with modernity, spills out into narrow, cobblestone streets and overflows from balconies draped with green plants and bright flowers. In the quiet siesta time, a village rests behind its intriguing doors.

In every town and tiny hamlet, I was captivated by the variety and character of entrance doors. Doors are kept from one generation to another, embellishments added, colors changed. Surely these doors reflect something of the family residing within and their stories. Some are playful and whimsical, some solemn and forbidding. Some look old and tired, as though they've withstood many battering storms. Still they stand guard over their family. Others are bright, cheerful, and almost invite you to come on in and sit down to visit awhile.

During siesta time, the towns shut down. The doors close up, and from two o'clock to five o'clock it's difficult to find anyone in town. Then at five, life sequestered behind the doors is resurrected, the doors open, and the commerce of living begins again. When I walked down the old streets in the evening, many doors were ajar. I grabbed every opportunity to take a look-see around. The door was open, after all, like an invitation to come in and share the life within. Often, the table and chairs inside are actually moved out into the street, and all individual lives in the town meld into one great river of life as neighbors eat and visit and children play with friends.

We all inhabit a space that is private and our very own. We all have doors that give a message to the world. *Do not enter. Do not disturb. Beware the bite.* Or, *Welcome. Come on in.* Some keep those doors closed much longer than others. And some hearts have doors that are always open wide, inviting pilgrims to step inside and share life.

The next morning, we left Belorado and climbed to the ridges of a mountain range. The "mountain" was not that high, but the path was narrow and steep. I wonder why Jesus did not depict the narrow road as also being steep? That would have conveyed additional difficulty. Walking a narrow *steep* trail is much harder than walking a narrow path.

Once we had reached the *alto,* the height of the ridge, our reward was a shady path through an area forested with beech, pine, and oak, a welcome change from the previous day's trail with little or no shelter from the sun.

Coming out of the trees and descending, we saw our destination, San Juan de Ortega, nestled in the valley with its church's triangular tower holding three bells and rising above all the other buildings. The village is named for St. John of the Nettle, a disciple of Santo Domingo, who also dedicated his life to aiding pilgrims by building roads and establishing a monastery here.

The church in San Juan offers an example of the intertwining of history and religion. At the top of one tall column reaching to the ceiling, a sculptured scene depicts the battle between the legendary French knight Roland and an evil giant. On another column we see the scene of the angel's visit to Mary, announcing the coming Baby.

Twice a year, a "Miracle of Light" occurs in this church. On both the spring and fall equinox, a beam of sunlight falls on and spotlights perfectly the Virgin Mary. These architectural wonders that came out of the medieval period impress me every bit as much as today's highly engineered structures.

We walked into San Juan to find that my guidebook's description of the town as *an isolated hamlet* was an understatement. The small huddle of buildings made a postage stamp look large. I checked the guidebook. *Pop. 20.* Of those 20 people, 19 were invisible when we arrived.

Although there is an albergue in San Juan, we decided we needed a more bustling metropolis and headed an additional mile and a half down the road to a place named Agés.

Agés had a population of 60. Most of them aged.

Our accommodations that night were at a place called *El Pajar* (the Hay Loft). All five of us were in one area, and as lights went out and we settled into our bunks, Grace said, "Simon, tell us a bedtime story."

Simon was a great storyteller. We listened in anticipation. And so he began.

He explained to us why paper curls.

Yes, that's right. This was his idea of a bedtime story. The man actually knew the scientific reason why a piece of paper will curl up. He went on and on and on. Something about friction, and this... and that... It was all mind-numbingly boring.

"Simon," I interrupted, "we need your stories every night—to put us to sleep!"

18

Beauty in His Cathedral

There could be no greater contrast than going from San Juan and Agés to the city of Burgos. As we walked the next day, we had several views of this metropolis waiting in the distance, spread out on the plain along a river, with the spires of its magnificent cathedral rising into the sky.

In 15 miles, we went from a hamlet of 60 to a city of 180,000.

Burgos is the second largest city on the Camino (the largest is Pamplona), and the main entry to the sprawling urban area from the Camino runs parallel to a four-lane highway and through the industrial part of town for almost ten kilometers. Coming from the pleasant small villages and relative peace of the countryside, the soul recoils as it faces this scene. Some pilgrims catch a bus on the outskirts of Burgos and ride into the city.

But once in the city, we found the beauty. The oldest part of town is still well-kept. The cathedral is said to be one of the most magnificent Gothic structures in Europe. Even with my uneducated eye for architecture and zero understanding of the correct terms, I was awed by the beauty, artwork, sculptures, and overall opulence of this place. Begun in the thirteenth century and built over a period of 300 years, the cathedral holds an overwhelming abundance of light, color, painstaking detail, and gold, lots of gold. Twenty-four small chapels are also a part of the cathedral, and any one of those surpasses the humble church serving 20 people in isolated San Juan.

Burgos, the magnificent Gothic city and San Juan, the remote, humble hamlet—these surely represent the greatest and the least of municipalities on the Camino de Santiago.

I cannot help but think about how we judge *the greatest* and *the least.*

This grand cathedral and impressive city did not exist when James the Apostle came to Spain, and we have no knowledge of whether or not he was ever in Burgos. But if he were to walk through San Juan and then Burgos today, I wonder if he would reflect back to a conversation Jesus had with His disciples.

Jesus and His small inner circle were walking down the road to Capernaum, and the conversation among the disciples descended into bickering. These handpicked men, those whom Jesus would rely on to carry on His work, were arguing about who was the most important in the group.

They were so like all of us. Each wanted to know that he was important in Jesus' ministry. There was rivalry and maybe a bit of jealousy. I'm sure James and John were involved in that discussion. We are told of another time when their mother came to Jesus privately and asked special favors for her sons. That sparked some dissension, too, when the rest of Jesus' circle heard about it.

Now the group was discussing the pecking order in their small organization. Everyone knew that Peter, James, and John were always invited along when Jesus did something special. They had just come down from a time with Him on the mountain—while all the other disciples had to wait below and deal with the crowds who wanted to see Jesus. Perhaps that's why there was a flare-up of rivalry on that day.

Jesus decided it was time to make a quick point of order. In today's lingo, He said something like, "Now see here, gentlemen." He drew a little child to His side.

"See this little child?"

They did. But surely they wondered what point Jesus was trying to make *with a child*. In their day and culture, children and women were on the lowest levels of social strata. Remember the time children came, wanting to see Jesus, and the disciples tried to hustle them away before they could "bother" Jesus?

"If you welcome this small boy in my name, you are also welcoming me and my Father, who sent me. In my Kingdom, it's not about being a big shot. The least one among you will now be the greatest. And you who always want to be first—you'll be last."

There He goes again, James might have thought. *Telling us we need to turn our thinking upside down. Setting His new guidelines that break all our paradigms.*

Well, okay, James didn't use that word, I'm sure. But He probably got the message: Toss out all your ideas about who is important and who is insignificant. God sees people in a very different way. And if you want to follow Jesus, there's no room for personal ambition.

I encountered Nick that day in a park in the city. Lori and I were going to meet there, but she was nowhere in sight when I arrived and saw the young man sitting alone on a bench. I sat down beside him, and with very little prompting he began to tell me his story.

His parents no longer sent money. He was broke and had to live on the generosity of others. A few days before, he and Simon had met locals who offered them a room in their own house, but most of the time Nick would find a barn or garage to sleep in. Simon kept buying him beer. Simon was still walking with us at this point, but in the coming days he and Nick would stop often to drink and fell farther and farther behind.

Nick was on the Camino because he did not know what else to do. He had no reason to go home. His parents were affluent, but he had no aspirations to follow in their profession. He had not found his spot in life, and the future looked blank and bleak. So he just kept walking.

"Nick," I told him. "You walked here from Amsterdam. You've already walked several thousand miles. You're living a story right now. Go back home, make yourself available to tell your story to groups, maybe even write a book about this adventure you're having."

He looked at me in surprise and with a faint hope.

"I could do that?" Apparently, he'd never even thought of doing such a thing to support himself.

Later that day, Nick visited the cathedral. Not because he was a believer, mind you. He had told me he didn't go to church and had no faith whatsoever. But—when you're in Burgos, you visit the magnificent, glittering cathedral.

In the evening, he told me that he had broken down and cried as he stood inside, surrounded by light and beauty.

"I don't know why," he said.

Well, I know why. He might have thought it was the soaring architecture and the intense beauty of the building, but the tears were not prompted by the stones and glass and gold. What moved Nick was a glimpse of something that he craves but does not have. Every person who doesn't have God is lacking something even if he or she does not know it. We created ones need a relationship with the God who created us and who created the beauty in that cathedral. Yes, I know men built the structure. But beauty in anything originates from God. *Beauty* was God's invention in the first place.

Something inside of every human being seeks something greater than itself. Sometimes no words are needed to get a glimpse of God. This was a cathedral built in the Middle Ages. We are told our bodies are living temples where the Spirit of God dwells, and if a medieval cathedral can touch a soul with God's beauty, then would it be possible for someone who doesn't believe in God to weep when he meets me, a living temple, and glimpses God alive in my life?

That was a question I asked myself that evening.

Lori, the Australian contingent, and I were staying at Divina Pastora, a hostel above a chapel with just 16 beds, all in one room. Word of mouth on the trail was that this was a special place to stay, but it filled up early. In busy Burgos, we had had a little trouble finding the chapel but managed to get there in time for all of us to reserve our beds. It was a good location, quite close to the cathedral.

Most of the albergues and hostels lock their doors at a set time each night. They also have a routine time in the morning when they unlock. This was occasionally inconvenient for us when we wanted to leave before dawn and the doors were still locked. Then there's also the time by which all occupants must be out, so they can clean and prepare for the new wave of pilgrims coming in that day.

Lori, Grace, Zoe, and I were already in our bunks. Simon had left as soon as we'd checked in that afternoon, and he was still out, drinking with Nick, who was staying elsewhere. The clock ticked toward lockup time, and Simon's bunk remained empty.

All of us were still awake, and someone started it. *Anyone want to wager on whether or not Simon will get back in time tonight?*

We all picked up on the joking, but there were no takers on the bet. Everyone was in agreement—tonight, Simon would be locked out.

We listened for his footsteps on the small, winding staircase that led up to our second-floor room. Nothing. The clock ticked on.

With one minute to go, the door downstairs opened and Simon came thundering up the stairs. It was obvious he'd had a little too much Nick and drink that evening.

Our friend slept undisturbed as we gathered our things to leave in the morning, and we would not see him again until Santiago.

19

Sunflowers on the Meseta

Hiking into Burgos through industrial areas had been dangerous and unpleasant; hiking out was an enjoyable walk in the light of the moon—at least, what little light penetrated the rain clouds above. In a light rain, through the quiet streets of the old part of the city, our footsteps fell where those of medieval pilgrims had also fallen. Then a short walk through parks and past the grounds of a modern university finally set us free of the city.

As the morning dawned, we began to meet the Meseta, the high plains between the mountain ranges that ring Spain.

The pilgrim's walk through the Meseta might seem at first glance like wilderness wanderings—shade is scarce; water fountains are farther between, and some of them are dry; towns are small, ancient, and offer only the pilgrim basics; and the grain fields and sky go on and on with no end in sight. The terrain is flat, and the sun is hot. Our guidebook warned us to fill our water bottles at every opportunity and to carry extra food. A pilgrim could never be sure of the next availability.

After a day of walking 13 miles through wheat fields and sheep droppings, we stopped in the hamlet of Hornillos del Camino, a centuries-old hamlet with a population of less than 75. The next planned stop was Castrojeriz, described in my guidebook as *a delightfully sleepy town with a declining population... who seem to be permanently occupied with siesta except during the garlic festival...*

Between Burgos and the next large city, León, we would walk about 180 kilometers (112 miles), and nearly every town has a "declining population." The population appears to be old and poor. Many of the young people are leaving Spain, looking for work, and these small villages are very likely kept alive by the older generations still there who provide for the needs of pilgrims.

The villages are rich in Camino history: castles and monasteries, small museums and churches abound. Even the towns with only a handful of residents have their stories to tell.

But between the towns, we walked. And walked. For a week, we walked toward an unchanging, unreachable horizon. Through endless fields. Under a vast sky.

My guidebook reads, *We might come across a shepherd and his flock or the occasional fox, otherwise you will have the birds to keep you company.*

We were on the second stage of the Camino de Santiago, the Meseta, and many people leave the trail here.

First, there are those who only hike part of the Camino as a holiday; they have limited time and their hearts are not necessarily set on pilgrimage. If you're going to choose only a part of the Camino, very few would choose the Meseta. Many leave the trail after arriving in Burgos.

Then there are those who do want to reach Santiago but catch a bus in Burgos and travel to the next large city, León. For many of these folks, hiking along through vast fields day after day simply looks too boring.

That's the word that's thrown about: *boring.* But could it be that these folks are simply afraid of the Meseta?

By this time, most pilgrims have pushed through their physical pains. They've figured out the best rhythm of walking and rest; they know what distances to plan for each day. The body is almost on autopilot, as I've described before, when everything moves together like a well-designed machine. The terrain is generally flat with few ascents, so there are few climbing challenges or changes in pace and necessary exertion. You no longer think about the weight on your back or whether you should be walking faster or slower. You've settled into your own hike, your body conditioned to do what it must do for this one day.

This is when the mind at rest suddenly feeds up things that you have been pushing down and refusing to think about. We do this all the time—we know there are issues we need to deal with and questions that need answers, but we procrastinate and keep ourselves busy with other things and push these issues to the back of our minds because we don't want to try to untangle things *now*.

But when you walk for hours a day, thinking and untangling is about all you have to do. And then you come face to face with those things within that you've been stubbornly ignoring. They bubble up and come to the surface, demanding attention and their rightful position and allotted time in your brain. Emotions, dilemmas, issues, questions—they're all brought out of the hidden recesses of the psyche and into immediate consciousness.

Many people are afraid of that. They're afraid to be alone too long, lest they have to face some of those things they've been avoiding. They're afraid of what will be discovered if suddenly all the busyness of their days is stripped away and they are just walking—just walking with their own thoughts.

The mountain trails can be excruciatingly difficult for bodies, but the Meseta will push and prod and stretch minds and emotions.

That is how it hit me. The sudden, overwhelming emotion ambushed me on a day I hiked alone.

In reality, there were few times when I did not see a pilgrim or two or three either in front or in back of me. But sometimes we walk alone in our pilgrimage. And sometimes, that aloneness is of our own choosing, because something deep inside needs the aloneness.

Of course, in aloneness we also risk an attack of loneliness. But even those attacks can be good for us. My experience has been that in the lonely times I can hear God speaking to me more plainly.

That day, I was walking alone and feeling especially lonely. Word had reached me that an aunt and uncle were both dying, and I was thinking about friends and family and how far away from them I was. I was thinking how *alone* I was on my pilgrimage, how insignificant I felt on these wide plains.

Then I came to the sunflower fields.

I had been watching the sunflower plants for days. In the early mornings when we left towns in the darkness, the sunflowers' heads were bowed low, awaiting the first rays of light. As the day brightened, the flowers perked up and turned their faces toward the sun rising in the sky, absorbing its light and energy all day. As evening fell and light faded, heads bowed low again, resting.

Early in my hike, the sunflowers had been bright and fresh and strong. Now, they were starting to lose the beautiful yellow crowns surrounding the seedy faces. The heads were not raised quite so strongly. Soon, these flowers would die.

That is, the plants die. But the seeds live on. The life they absorbed goes on in oil or bird food or snacks we enjoy. Or the seeds bring forth a new generation of sunflowers.

We ought to be more like the sunflower, with our heads bowing in reverence to God and our faces turned toward the Son who gives life and strength.

On that lonely day in the sunflower field, I thought about the folks in my life who have been like those flowers. They had absorbed God's light and then passed on, leaving behind the seeds of more light and life. I thought of my grandmother, who had meant so much to us. A young lad of just 15 who passed away one tragic night. A godly grandfather who influenced generations of his own lineage and hundreds of strangers. Aunts and uncles who have left this earth: Elizabeth, Sara, Anna, Henry, Marion, and Roman. My thoughts came to my own mom and dad. Dad was 89, a sunflower that had lost some of its golden crown. He has soaked up the light of the Son for years, and now the energy slowly ebbs from him. Other uncles were still with us: John, David, and Andrew.

Many folks are fortunate to have one sunflower in their lives. I have had an entire field of them.

When this awareness struck me, a strange and totally unexpected thing happened.

I wept.

I rarely do that, but on that day in the sunflower fields, there was no stopping it. I cried like a baby, blubbering and snotting along for several miles. I cried so much that I warned myself to drink more water—I needed to rehydrate.

The overwhelming emotion was gratitude. Why was I so fortunate, so blessed, to benefit from all these people who had spent their lives soaking up God's rays and then leaving those seeds of goodness and kindness behind to bless and encourage me? *Why me, God?*

God didn't give me an answer. I saw a town in the distance, and I blinked and squinted and sniffed, so that when my tired feet reached the outskirts of town, they were accompanied by a dry face.

When I can no longer lift my head, and, like the sunflower plant, I wither away and pass from the earth, will the seeds I leave be a blessing?

I blogged about that time of loneliness and tears in the sunflower field. Lori did not know of this breakdown until she read about it on my blog. Then she apologized for not being with me. But, she added, it was probably during a time she was also hiking alone and crying her own tears.

20
T-roads

Under that wide, vast sky, we walked and walked and walked. Day after day for a week. Through grain and hay and sunflower fields. Past lines of wind turbines and flocks of sheep. Over flat terrain broken occasionally by a gentle hill. Resting at night in ancient pilgrim towns.

In one town, we met Liz, a young lady from Germany who had just graduated from college. She was very smart, engaged to be married, and had plans to be a doctor. We would hike with her off and on the rest of the way to Santiago, and although she spoke fluent English, she and I dialogued in German, just for fun.

It was always good to see familiar faces, either at cafés, in the hostels, or on the trail. We connected numerous times with the two Scottish ladies we had met in Pamplona, Beth and

Alice. They were having a good time on their adventure together without the husbands. The Australians Grace and Zoe walked with us at times, but although we occasionally called Simon to see where he was and he always predicted he would catch up with us, he never appeared.

We stopped one morning for breakfast at the albergue at San Bol, a small structure alongside the road in a grove of trees. The hostel has only twelve beds, and communal meals are served at a large, round table under a domed roof. At this spot there is also a spring which has healing powers, according to legend. Water running from a stone façade built around the spring was collected in a trough, and these waters are said to be especially good to ease the aching of feet.

I thought I should have some of this elixir in my water bottle. Lori looked at me in disbelief, horrified that I'd even think of drinking the water where folks might have soaked their aching extremities. She was also certain that, besides human debris floating around, there would be fish and snakes and other wiggly creatures in the water. I couldn't argue with her; it was all probably true of the water in the trough.

I went to the source, instead, the place where the fresh spring water fell from the stones, and filled my bottle there.

Another stop was at the ruins of an ancient convent. Actually, we walked through the ruins—the Camino path took us under a splendid archway that was part of the complex. In medieval days, bread was left in the alcoves of this arch for the sustenance of pilgrims passing through. Now a small hostel has also been built there, making use of some of the walls that still stand.

In Castrojeriz, Zoe and I climbed a hill to visit a castle built in the ninth century. Although crumbling at places, the ruins still command the entire countryside, towering imperiously over the town. From that prominence, we had a fantastic view of the plains, with small hills rising here and there and looking like mounds of sand rising from the brown valley floor.

In one of the larger towns, I again attended mass. Again, I waited for the communion. And again, the announcement came that it was only for practicing Catholics. I did participate, though, in receiving the blessing of the pilgrims.

We walked and walked. We took off our shoes at the end of the day and nursed tired feet; we washed our clothes in sinks and hung them on lines to dry quickly in the hot air; we sat around supper tables with folks from all over the world and communicated even without shared language; we tried to shut out the snoring and other hostel night sounds; and we got up in the morning and put on our shoes again and walked. And walked.

All the while, the fabric of my pants continued to pull apart further and further. My needle and thread were gone. At one hostel, I did ask for more mending supplies and sat down in a very public area trying to sew the tear (yes, with my pants on), hoping to lure someone into offering assistance.

But no one came to my aid. Those great North Face pants now have quite a colorful assortment of threads in stitches of all sizes, pointing in all directions.

On the sixth day traversing the Meseta, we took a morning break in the larger town of Sahagún. Sitting outside a little café with our breakfast and coffee, we were happy to see Grace and Zoe walking down the street. Zoe had been sick a few days before and they had stayed behind. Now they'd taken a taxi to catch up with us.

The Scottish ladies were there too, laughing and having a ball, as usual. They had been doing the Camino for a number of years, walking a section and then going home, to return and complete another section the next year.

Liz was also there, and she was studying the guidebook. We had a decision to make, she informed us.

Shortly beyond Sahagún, the path splits. The guidebook actually lists two different towns as optional destinations for the next night. We had made plans to stay in Calzadilla de los Hermanillos, but Liz had heard about an albergue in Bercianos del Real Camino that served a communal meal and she wanted to stay there.

Either choice was fine with me. I didn't care which way we went, as long as we were headed toward Santiago. I will admit, though, that a communal pilgrim meal was always an enticement for me.

But what might we miss on the other path? That question did occur to me. Even in life, I find myself questioning decisions. *What might happen if I choose this way? What will I miss if I don't go that way?* At times, if we aren't careful, we can find our progress bogged down or even stalled completely by the indecision.

Ever hear someone say they are at a crossroads in life and need to make a difficult choice? I've probably used that metaphor myself. But one day it dawned upon my feeble brain that this comparison is in error. At a crossroads, one doesn't actually need to choose a different path. One can choose to continue on the same path they have been traveling. Not making a choice of direction, simply sailing along as we have always done is, in essence, making a choice. We go wherever the road takes us, and we leave our destiny up to someone or something else.

I live in Amish Country and traverse many back roads. Some are what we call T-roads, where the road literally ends as it connects to another road. At the intersection of these roads, a definite choice must be made—do I go left or right?

Our T-roads demand a decision, and the choice of direction determines where we will end up that day. So it is with life. Even small choices shape our destiny.

Is that the reason we are sometimes frozen in place? Are we paralyzed because we want desperately to know what lies in either direction? If I go left, what will I miss by not going right? Or we postpone our decision until we have thoroughly weighed the advantages and disadvantages of each direction. This is akin to pulling up a chair and sitting by the roadside until your beard grows to the ground or your unshaved legs look like the wheat field ahead of you. There you sit, watching the world pass by, never actually knowing what lies down the highway to either the left or the right—until suddenly one day you realize that while you've been watching and pondering, the roads have been rerouted and you've missed whatever opportunities were waiting in either direction. There you still sit, alongside the abandoned road, with your only company the straggly weeds pushing up through the cracks in the pavement.

I suppose there is one more option. With my four-wheel drive I could plow straight ahead at the T-road, crashing through the fence and continuing down the farmer's corn or wheat field—but that would be lunacy. However, isn't that lunacy exactly what we sometimes indulge in, as we insist on going straight ahead when what is called for is a life-altering change of direction?

Make a decision! Get involved in your own destiny. Choose a direction. Take a risk, and go down the path that frightens you the most. You will be amazed at what you discover. You will finally discover the real you. You may even end up admiring that person you find.

Well, this wasn't a T-road in Spain, it was a Y-road. Still, there was a decision to be made.

To tell the truth, that day I cared very little about all of that wise advice I just gave you on making decisions. I was sitting by the roadway, observing life. I did not care which way we went.

Perhaps the Meseta was getting the best of me. For many kilometers and many hours I'd done nothing but think about home. What was I missing there? Choosing to chase this adventure, I had plucked myself up, out of the fabric of family and community life and isolated myself from everyone important to me. And for what? Walking through grain fields? Was I even missed? I was beginning to feel very melancholy.

The group made the decision, and we headed toward the albergue promising a communal meal.

I could go back and hike that other path someday, but it will never be the same again. On this journey, our choices each day determine the people we meet and the experiences we have. I can never recapture that day and what I might have missed the first time—in this journey, you don't get many do-overs.

That's why we need to enjoy whatever path we've chosen for today and not waste a moment looking back and lamenting what we might be missing. Instead, let's enjoy what we are living.

However, that day I was lamenting.

21

Transformation

Most pilgrims who walk the entire Camino will tell you that the pilgrimage is a life-changing experience. Not all walkers are seeking spiritual answers, miracles, or healing. Some admit they are looking for something but don't know what that something is. Some walk the Camino simply for the experiences they have along the way. But regardless of the reason for coming to the Way of Saint James, most people are changed in one way or another.

I have three stories of transformation for you. Whether or not they have any connection, I will let you decide.

Let's start with the shortest story.

Every now and then, we saw a couple who were always holding hands. Walking, eating, sightseeing, they were always thus attached. Observing them might have been what triggered a conversation I had with Grace one day about love and her husband. I had noticed that Grace talked with hubby on the phone several times a day.

Grace's husband had tried to kill himself.

He had been depressed, she told me, and one day she found him hanging in their small shop, red-faced and gasping. She called for help and gave him mouth-to-mouth resuscitation.

He recovered, and when he realized what she had done for him, his character was completely changed. Now, he was kind and sweet and supportive. (Apparently, he had lacked these qualities in his previous life.)

"You know," I told Grace, "that's exactly what Christians believe about the old man dying and Christ giving us a new life. We're new people. He gives us qualities we never possessed on our own. Your husband hung the old man, and a new man came out of it."

Grace (who as far as I know was not a believer) was thoughtful. She may have the best illustration of God's transformative power living right in front of her.

We call the second story the Transfiguration.

Jesus invited Peter, James, and John along to a mountain retreat for a prayer meeting. Once Jesus started praying, His face lit up and His clothes, according to Luke, were as bright as a lightning flash.

In spite of witnessing all this glory, Peter, James, and John fell asleep. They must have been startled to awaken and find that, from out of nowhere, two more men had appeared—two men that were presumed dead. Death had been kind to these two—Moses and Elijah were also adorned in splendor.

From what James, John, and Peter could ascertain, the conversation centered on what was about to happen to Jesus when He reached Jerusalem. As the conversation drew to a close, Peter—in the understatement of the ages—remarked that he felt it was good for them to have been there. He offered to build three shelters or tents of worship, one for Jesus, one for Elijah, and one for Moses. You have to hand it to Peter; he wasn't concerned about himself; he was looking out for his friend Jesus. Luke does mention that Peter was so befuddled he didn't know what he was saying.

While Peter was talking, the shadow of a cloud came over them. It must have been a massive, intimidating cloud, because it soon enveloped them completely and sent bolts of terror through the men. Peter must have been regretting his impulsive words.

Then, from within the cloud, came a voice.

Now we all know that some folks claim they've heard from God. Let me tell you, these boys really did hear from God that day. The message was short and to the point.

"This is my Son, whom I have chosen," the voice said. "Listen to Him."

The message hasn't changed much over the years. As a matter of fact, it hasn't changed a bit. When God speaks to us through His Holy Word, the message still resonates. *This is my Son. Listen to Him.*

Do you? Will you?

While Jesus and His inner circle were having their mountaintop experience, the remainder of the disciples were grappling with their own dilemma—not very successfully, sad to say. A father had brought his son to them. The boy was afflicted with an evil spirit that caused the child to scream and go into spastic convolutions.

The father begged the disciples to drive the demon out of the boy. They could not do it. Can you imagine the frustration they felt? Why should they have to handle this? Where was Jesus?

As Jesus came down the mountain and the father went to seek His help, the demon made one final stand of desperation and violently flung the boy to the ground.

Jesus took one look at the awful situation and admonished the evil seed to be gone.

The crowd that had gathered around was amazed at what they had just witnessed. Jesus, meanwhile, called the disciples together for a listen-up-guys-and-listen-carefully meeting. What He had to say was of utmost importance.

"It's been set in motion. I'm going to be betrayed and handed over to the enemy."

While the disciples didn't grasp the true meaning of this, they caught the sense of impending evil, and were filled with fear.

One would think that after their mountaintop experience, Peter, James, and John would still be filled with the radiance of Jesus and the thrill of hearing God's voice. They had seen Moses and Elijah. They had been given a glimpse into the heavenly realm. They had heard eternal beings discussing events to come. Wouldn't that transform your outlook if these things happened to you?

Yet there they were, afraid of what lay ahead. Too afraid, even, to ask Jesus to explain it further.

James the apostle, known as St. James by the Catholic Church, was every bit as human as we are.

We tend to forget that. We think of the disciples of Jesus as holy, devout men, but they bickered and doubted and waffled just as we do. Even Jesus' three closest friends, after being given a glimpse into heavenly realms and hearing God's voice from that realm, came down off the mountain and were beset by fear and lack of faith.

Even so, Jesus had high expectations for this motley group. What made it possible for them to carry the Gospel to all nations, to the ends of the earth? What made it possible for them to perform miracles, mere humans that they were? What made it possible for James to stick to the mission, even when it meant his death?

Could it have been their obedience to the one they followed?

We all have our struggles, too. Everyone's journey is filled with ups and downs. Can our obedience turn our pilgrimage here on earth into a miracle accomplishing God's purposes?

Story Three.

It usually happens at some point on my excursions. I forget how fortunate I am to be traveling, doing and seeing things many folks only dream of. I am sort of like Peter, taking his eyes off Jesus while walking on the water. He focused on the turbulent elements and his own precarious situation instead of realizing the wonder all around.

So it was with me, that afternoon as we walked into Bercianos del Real Camino, headed toward the albergue that Liz had selected. The elements have taken a toll on these buildings of stucco, and many are crumbling. The bright flowers that other towns had worn like jewels were absent here. We saw windows stuffed with old straw and mud. Immediately, I gave this town a name, the "ugly town." There was a depressing feel to the place.

I now realize I was the one traveling under a depressing cloud, like—who was it in the old *Peanuts* cartoons? Pigpen? Remember him? He was always shrouded in a cloud of dirt. That was me that day as I walked into the drab town. I was sick of the Camino. *I don't want to be here. I want to be home.*

The negative words clicked through my mind, keeping time with my hiking sticks: sad, lonely, depressed, bored. I may not have said the words consciously to myself, but every thought came out of that well of gloom and self-pity.

We had arrived during siesta time and the burgeoning population of 200 was ensconced in the drab houses. Some of the towns we walked through were drab, but when people are mingling about, the place has a soul. This town was currently soulless and my soul was drab.

We found our albergue, a big square building. The old brown bricks looked as though they had been smeared with mud to hold everything together. Some corners were crumbling, and a few windows actually were covered with black bars.

What? We're staying here?

We'd arrived early enough that we could not even check in. Most hostels have a certain time they open in the afternoon. We sat on a bench in front of the building and waited.

Once we did check in, the Scottish ladies, Lori, Grace, Zoe, and I walked downtown—if you can call it a *downtown* when there's less than 200 people—and looked for a place to get something to eat. But it was siesta time. The town was dead.

Finally, on a little side street, we found a bar that was open. Inside, the place was empty except for the bartender. We ordered our food and sat outside. During the hours we killed time there, only two other men came in. I focused on my iPad, doing blogs, reading the news, answering emails. I just wanted to be away from the whole Camino scene. I was done, ready to go home. And I knew that God was not sending a bus to pick me up this time.

Suppertime arrived, and we gathered for the communal meal. Sometime during the evening, a streak of pain went through my left leg. I looked down, but saw nothing. *Probably a fly bite*, I thought.

After the meal, some of the volunteers at the hostel led singing. They had written their own lyrics (in Spanish) about life in a hostel, and accompanied by a guitar, they led the group in attempting a rendition sung to the tune of "La Bomba." I understood none of the words, but the tune brought back memories.

Then someone announced that it was the birthday of one of the pilgrims. They sang "Happy Birthday." That started a marathon of happy-birthdaying. We sang the cheerful little ditty in the native language of each country represented in the room—or at least, those who knew the language sang. All who knew German sang in German; those who spoke French sang in French; our English tongues sang the words we all knew. With over 30 people there, we sang at least six or seven versions of the song. And after every rendition, the group cheered and clapped and congratulated themselves on a fine concert. Everyone else was having a great time.

My leg was beginning to itch.

Finally, it was time to do dishes. But one of the volunteers offered an alternative. "Anyone want to go out and watch the sun set instead of cleaning up?"

Well, sure. I was so bored and discontented that I considered a sunset would be more exciting than anything else I had done that day.

We set out, walking to a nearby knoll from which we'd have a good view of the western sky. My thigh was now on fire. *A fly bite would not hurt this much, would it?*

Climbing to the crest of the hill, we stood above a vast plain. The sky was a dark blue with wisps of clouds drifting with the breeze. Way out in the distance, the golden orb slipped toward the dark horizon. A gentleman seated nearby on a picnic table was playing a lilting tune on a flute.

Bored, depressed, and lonely, I had walked into a scene that instantly strummed all my emotions. The notes of the flute transported me back to the summer of '08, on the final leg of my Appalachian Trail hike.

The previous day I had hiked from Rangeley, Maine, to the Spaulding Mountain shelter, slogging through 19 miles of mud and mountain climbs. The weather was cold and rainy. I arrived at Spaulding Mountain shelter and quickly set up my tent.

Some distance behind me was Padre, the Catholic priest. A stronger hiker than I, he could usually catch up with me by day's end. Not on this miserable day. He only made it as far as Lone Mountain, still two miles short of my tent site. Darkness was setting in, and he set up camp quickly. He was what we called a hammock hanger. He slept in a hammock, swaying between two trees. (This style of bed was an advantage in crowded shelters; he could suspend the hammock from trusses and sleep levitated over the rest of us.) On that night, he stretched his hammock atop Lone Mountain and spent a long sleepless night swaying in the wind and rain. He nearly froze that night.

As I prepared to leave the following morning, I met Padre rushing toward the shelter. He'd warm up some food, he said, and then catch up with me.

I was struggling up Spaulding Mountain a while later, bent over with the pack on my back. I wanted nothing more than to get through the next 250 miles of my hike and finally go home.

That's when the music came. Padre carried a flute with him on the trail, and now the clear notes came floating over the mountain side. I paused mid-stride and listened... and imagined. In my mind's eye I could see Padre seated on the shelter floor with flute in hand.

The notes dropping through the trees and mist spoke to my spirit. They spoke of the healing I had found after the loss of my wife. Here in the wilderness, I had also been given the peace I'd prayed for, and the music told of that. The melody, coming out of nowhere and wrapping around me, also brought the realization that the hike would soon be over. What then? Then I would suffer another loss—I would part with the people and the trail that had become my life.

The haunting notes floated across the mountain that misty morning and penetrated the walls that guard my emotions. I leaned out over my hiking stick and wept freely. The last vestiges of grief and loss were poured out on the Maine mountainside, and as that emptied out of me, clarity came. I saw how the difficulty of the hike had obscured the joy of the day-to-day journey. I saw that this one moment in the Maine woods was a treasured thing, with Padre's notes dropping gently around me and the truth of the trail clear before my eyes.

From a Spain hillside, we watched the magnificence of God's creation, a brilliant gift of color and, yes, serenity as He put the Meseta to rest for the day. The notes from the flute dropped around me and once again brought back the message: *This is a special moment. Savor it now.*

My flagging spirits rose, and, like that moment on the Maine mountain, clarity came again.

The pilgrimage is long and often so hard. But God's goodness gives us gifts in every moment. Look for them. Enjoy them.

Here I was, doing what I love—walking. Instead of getting up and going to work, I get to do this. I get to watch God's sun set in Spain. *In Spain!* I get to do it with neat people from all over the world who can sing "Happy Birthday" in seven different languages.

I had been lost and disoriented for a while, focusing too much on what I did not have. On that knoll of transformation, I was given a fresh look at all that I have been given.

My friend whose trail name is "Hoosier" reminds me that the Christian life is not easy. There are lots of ups and downs, just like on the trail. But every day, we have to get up and believe there is a destination and that we will see it eventually if we keep going.

Perhaps that glimpse into the heavenly realm did change James. Perhaps that was why he could stick with the mission so determinedly—even when it meant his life was on the line. He believed in that realm he had seen and in the final destination.

When we are given the new life that God's Spirit brings alive within us, we are also given new eyes to catch those glimpses when God pulls back the curtains of Heaven for a few moments, and we're given new ears to hear the notes of His voice—both reminders that we have a final home where Jesus blazes in His glory and God makes things whole and perfect.

We come down from our mountains of transfiguration and find that we still battle doubt and fear and our old natures, but we keep our hearts set on pilgrimage—because we've had a glimpse of our destination.

> But the people of God will sing a song of joy,
> like the songs at the holy festivals.
> You will be filled with joy,
> as when a flutist leads a group of pilgrims
> to Jerusalem, the mountain of the Lord—
> to the Rock of Israel.
> (Isaiah 30:29)

A thousand ants swarmed over my left leg that night, every one of them taking a morsel of my flesh as sustenance for their journey. At least, that's the way my skin felt. For days and nights, my leg would either go numb or burn as though every nerve end had been prodded awake. Sometimes the feverish feeling in my thigh was almost unbearably hot. There was no pattern to the onset of this discomfort; it came during the night and while I was walking on the trail.

Since I returned from Spain, I've done some research and diagnosed the problem as a spider bite. Apparently Spain hosts several arachnids that can be deadly, and I am fortunate that the only lingering effect I've had is a slight numbness of my thigh that still comes and goes intermittently. If there is poison lingering in my body, it has not moved upward to my brain—at least, not that I'm aware of... aware of... aware of...

22

A Cathedral and a Simple Life

One more day across the dry, remote countryside brought us to Mansilla de las Mulas, where each pilgrim is faced with a decision. Twelve miles ahead lies the large city of León, and walking into the busy town was said to be even more dangerous than entry into Burgos. For a number of kilometers, the pilgrim's path runs along a traffic-filled, four-lane highway. The outskirts of the town are lined with factories and car dealerships.

Aside from the physical dangers awaiting walkers who navigate their way in such close proximity to speeding cars and trucks, there is the vulnerability of the soul to this industrialized and commercial environment. After the relative calm and serenity of the country lanes, walking here is nerve-wracking.

There is yet another difficulty. In any city, the scallop shells marking the path are more difficult to spot. They are often embedded in the street, and with many streets converging and much pedestrian traffic and various diversions all serving to both distract the pilgrim's attention and also to obscure the waymarking—well, it's easy for a pilgrim to lose his way in the cities. Surely there is a spiritual allegory in there somewhere.

Many folks do take a bus from Mansilla de las Mulas into León. Some do so out of concern for personal safety, others climb on a bus because of physical issues at this point, and still others are simply bored and want to be finished with the Meseta as quickly as possible.

Of course, I could not and would not take the bus.

León was a landmark for me in several ways. First, I felt I had earned a stay in one of the upscale Parador hotels, so I had made a reservation there and was looking forward to the luxury of a modern facility and a fantastic breakfast buffet.

Then, too, arriving in León meant I was beyond the halfway point of my hike. More miles lay behind me than ahead of me.

We ate supper with the Australians and Alice and Beth. The Scottish duo would be leaving the Camino the next day. I said goodbye to them with some regret, wishing I had spent more time in getting to know them better. These two ladies had been friends most of their lives, and they were certainly enjoying life. I suppose their husbands at home were having fun as well. Most of my adventures have been solitary. Aloneness is lonely and actually quite good for a person if done in moderation. Loneliness makes us appreciate our family and friends and reminds us not to take them for granted. (Of course, I am guilty of coming home and slowly slipping back into old ways and once again sinking into unexpressed appreciation.) But I watched the fun Alice and Beth were having as they shared this experience, and I was keenly aware that the person with whom I had once shared my experiences and stories was now gone. Mary and I had dreamed of *someday...* and then our plans were cut short. I must reiterate that message I took to the Appalachian Trail: Enjoy and appreciate your loved ones while you have them.

Another face had joined our Camino days. We had met Angelina the previous night. She was from Germany, and our paths would cross occasionally all the way to the end of the earth.

León has much to see and do. Besides being the current capital of the province of León, the city holds a great deal of history, a connection to people and events that have been pivotal to this area of Spain. As usual in these cities, the pilgrims' journey is focused on the medieval part of town, but the entire city is a tourist destination. There are old monasteries and churches, museums, Gothic palaces, and many plazas and parks with fountains and statues.

Here in León, I thought again of Nick and his tears in the Burgos cathedral. The Catedral Pulchra Leonina in León is amazing. I strolled through the interior, enraptured by the light filtering through 125 stained glass windows high in the walls and ceiling of the cathedral. Shimmering, glimmering fragments of deep color danced all around me as the sun's rays passed through the shards of colored glass. I stood in awe, staring at the windows and the patterns of color on the stone floor, the walls, and even on my own body. I thought of how God's light shines through the stained and broken pieces of our lives and makes it possible for beauty—created only by Him—to emanate from us.

The cathedral also seemed like a tiny preview of Heaven. The Bible describes the walls surrounding the celestial city as being made of jasper, on foundations of emeralds and sapphires and other colorful gems. As I near that city, will I walk in even more awe of its beauty and grandeur as the Son shines through and His light meets me?

As I contemplated an image of Baby Jesus on His mother's lap, one beam of light came through a window and for a few brief seconds fell directly on the One who was born to bring light and life to the dark world.

The Camino led us onward. After leaving León, we found our path sheltered more often by trees, and soon we were walking past corn fields. The change was welcome, after days of looking at wheat and sunflowers and already-harvested, brown fields. The smell of the ripening corn evoked memories of home.

On days like this, not much happened. I just walked and observed God's world and the corn grew.

Life was simple.

This simplicity of life and the contentment that can accompany it was pictured for me that night in Villavante. We had supper at the albergue of Santa Lucía. Some towns have no restaurants or bars, and so the hostel cooks a meal for those who order it at check-in. After supper, I noticed that across the street the old folks were gathering. In front of an ancient building, senior citizens of the town sat on benches and talked and laughed all evening. This is the night life in such small hamlets. Many of the young people are gone.

But for the folks over there on the benches, life did not appear to be measured by what they owned or the external entertainment available to them. Contentment seemed simple.

23

A Sunday's Walk

Streaks of gold, pink, and purple lit up the eastern skies the next morning as we approached Puente de Órbigo. Here one of the longest medieval bridges in Spain spans the river and leads into town. The bridge is called the Passage of Honor, a lofty title arising from a strange story. Apparently, back in 1434, a certain knight had been seen around town wearing an iron collar. This was a symbol of his condition—he was a "prisoner of love." His unknown beloved apparently did not return his affection, and thus the burden of the iron ring.

    I suppose he eventually got tired of dragging it around. But honor, of course, made it impossible to simply take the thing off and put it in a drawer. No, there must be some noble way of ridding himself of this imprisonment and re-establishing his knightly honor.

And thus we have him standing on the bridge, blocking the way of all who would pass. Accounts differ. (I suppose it's understandable that the story has undergone some alterations over the last six centuries.) Some say he boasted of his skill and invited all knights to tournaments of jousting. Other accounts say he stopped all pilgrims on their way to Santiago, gave them a horse, a lance, and armor and challenged them to battle their way over the bridge. If they refused to fight, they were forced to wade across the river. Eventually, by some unknown rule of honor, he ascertained that breaking 300 lances had finally set him free of the iron chains of love, his honor was reestablished, and he left the bridge and undertook a pilgrimage to Santiago, where he placed a gold necklace around the neck of the image of one of the saints in the cathedral.

Another account (which I prefer) is that everyone got tired of the whole silly thing—he was quite a disruption to the town's traffic, of course—and a group of knights banded together and confronted him on the long span, whereupon they simply offered to break their own lances to speedily move him to that 300 mark and have the thing over and done with.

A strange story indeed. Yet I have to wonder—how many of our rituals and societal behaviors today might seem equally odd or foolish to folks who will come after us?

As the sun rose above the horizon and full day broke, we passed through the town without one lovesick and pugnacious knight handing over a lance and challenging me to a joust.

It was Sunday morning, a beautiful morning with a blue sky arched over us and white clouds drifting slowly across the blue. I was in church—God's cathedral of nature. Grace and Lori were ahead of me, chatting and oblivious to this worship time. I walked alone, thinking.

As if to accompany my pensive mood, church bells rang out over the countryside.

We walked through farmland. The terrain here was fairly flat, with only small undulating slopes looking like gentle waves of the sea. The cadence of the bells rolled out over the fields, coming from a scattering of red-tiled roofs on a hillside almost a mile away.

By the time we reached the edge of the village, the bells had stopped and a chorus of voices sang words I could not recognize. It did not matter; the music reached out and embraced pilgrims and drew us in, welcoming us and making us a part of Sunday morning in Santibáñez de Valdeiglesia.

The song grew louder and the music more compelling as I entered the streets that lay quietly under the drifting melody. Strangely, no hikers were ahead of me and no villagers were out and about. It seemed I was a lone pilgrim. Then, as I neared the source of the music, four elderly people came from a dirt side street and walked ahead of me, two of them leaning on their canes. I passed them and continued on toward the music.

An albergue came into view, with a few pilgrims loitering outside. Next to the albergue, almost hidden behind the more prominent building, was a small stone church. Its walls were almost windowless and the steeple rose above the neighboring buildings. Three bells hung in the triangular tower, a design I'd come to recognize. The music that had drawn me into town emanated from the depths of this stone sanctuary.

In John's vision of Heaven, he heard choirs singing. That morning, with the images of brilliant light from the León cathedral still in my mind, I imagined what it might be like when I come to the crest of that final hill on my road to Heaven. As I have hiked, the music will have called to me from a distance long before I see the city. It encourages me onward. At last I top the hill and see the city before me, with the light from within shimmering through the beautiful walls of clear jasper. I quicken my steps. The closer I get, the stronger the music becomes. It welcomes me, pulling me home. I look ahead, eagerly, and I see at the gates made of pearl my loved ones waiting to greet me.

Dry and dusty farmland stretched out before and behind us, and the reddish soil of the fields was barely discernible from the dirt road under our feet. Out in the middle of nowhere, we came upon a fruit stand appearing like an oasis in a brown desert. For a donation, we were invited to partake of numerous fruits and fruit juices. It was a welcome break. I made a donation and partook.

On a cushion in the shade of an overhang extending from the dilapidated building sat the tall Asian man we had first seen in Belorado. He seemed to be an integral part of the configuration of the building, and I assumed he was staying there. His guitar leaned against a large sun painted on the wall.

The next short stop was at a stone cross on a hill overlooking the city of Astorga. In this city, the French Camino (which I was walking) merges with another Camino coming from the south. The city was founded in the first century by the Romans, long before anyone was making pilgrimages to Santiago, and it's been an important crossroads of commerce for centuries. Beyond Astorga we could see mountains—the mountains of Galicia, our third and final section of the Camino.

A large, modern albergue welcomes pilgrims at the edge of Astorga, and across the street a municipal hostel provides more accommodations. But one of the Germans hiking with us had told Lori about a good restaurant serving vegetarian food—close to the cathedral at the opposite end of town, he said. Anytime our little grass-eater heard a rumor of vegetarian meals, she made a beeline for said eating establishment. Now she was determined she was going to head to that side of the city. I was okay with this choice, since our guidebook assured us we would find another hostel there, a historic building in the old quarter that had been converted into a pilgrim hostel. As for supper, I thought perhaps I could order a dish of alfalfa.

We walked more than a kilometer, and still there was no sight of a hostel, much less a vegetarian restaurant. I had thought I caught a glimpse of what looked like the building we were seeking down a side street, but Lori and I had a slight disagreement about exactly *where* this place was supposed to be, and we passed the street and soldiered on. We were nearing the far edge of the city, so we finally stopped a woman and asked if she might know how we could get to San Javier, the hostel. She could not speak English, but she attempted to communicate with much pointing and waving of hands. We could not understand this communication either—she was pointing in all directions. We gave up, and I finally convinced Lori to turn around. Otherwise, we would still be walking, because if there is a vegetarian restaurant to be found, Lori will not stop until we are seated within.

We asked for directions from another person who seemed more knowledgeable and eventually did find San Javier.

After checking in and having my *credencial* stamped, I grabbed the necessities and headed to the shower room. It was a long hallway with the stalls lining one wall. I went down the row to the very end and entered the last shower.

Observing the normal routines for showers, I undressed and hung my clothes on the hook. Then I turned the water on and stepped under the spray. I lathered up.

Boom! The shower head blew off, shot across the small space, and went rolling under the door of the stall.

The stream of water that now pummeled my body hit with the force of a sandblaster, threatening to shred my skin. It was impossible to shower under this. I quickly turned off the flow.

Now what? I'm in the middle of a shower, covered with soap.

I need that shower head.

Opening the stall door, I peered out. I could hear that other folks were in other showers, but no one appeared in the hallway. In sudsy nakedness, I stepped out of the stall and took a quick glance around the hallway. No shower head presented itself.

It had to be somewhere.

My ears stayed alert for the sound of water ceasing to run in the other showers.

I spied a set of steel shelves along the end wall. The lowest shelf was far enough above the floor that a fugitive shower head might have taken cover there. Down on my hands and knees I went, peering under the shelves and into the corners.

There it sat, taunting me.

I reached out and grabbed it and hustled back to the safety of the shower stall where I attached it tightly in its proper spot and finished my shower without further incidents.

24

Learning to Believe

The town was celebrating that day. I do not know what the occasion was, but it called for dancing and music in the streets.

Many times, we were witnesses of or participants in these types of festivities. Town squares came alive with music, joyfulness, and laughter. On this day, it seemed to be a music fair. Bands played and acrobats tumbled about. Children were everywhere, trying out unusual instruments set up for them to play with and produce rhythmic music. One invention was constructed of corrugated pipe and played with a flip flop. Pots and pans made great percussion instruments. The music went on all afternoon as I wandered about the streets and found something to eat.

Later that evening, Liz and I sat outside the albergue with our feet soaking in a trough of salt water provided for pilgrims. She had not yet eaten, so I offered to go with her, and back to the town square we went.

Along the way, we met two German men we had hiked with. Liz knew them better than I did—they shared a common homeland.

"We're going down to the square to get a bite to eat."

"We'll go with you."

So we two became four.

Around the next corner we went and soon encountered two more pilgrims who were also invited to come with us. Lori joined us at some point. We Pied-Pipered our way along the street, and by the time we reached the square and found a table, our group numbered 13. We ate and talked and watched the festivities, simply enjoying the light-hearted spirit of the evening.

Sitting next to me was a petite, dark-eyed Spanish girl named Judit. She had walked in with a tall man who looked Hispanic. Bearded, graying, fifty-ish, he conversed with Judit in Spanish and I guessed him to be her father. He was sitting down the table from me, and we did not have a conversation, yet I thought I had him figured out. He was a bit arrogant and cocky, I decided.

But Judit was a delightful young woman who seemed to be an intelligent, dedicated Christian. She carried an aura about her, a calmness of spirit, even though when she was excited, she talked fast and her English words sometimes got all tangled up and tumbled over each other. Having just graduated, she wanted to do something with her life that

LEARNING TO BELIEVE 175

would help people and make a difference in the world. She did not have a lot of money, but she told me about a child in India she supported. Judit works with primary school children and teaches English to older youth after school. She would tell me later, "They are awesome. They are the ones who teach me."

As I watched a little girl dancing a toddler's dance, it reminded me that Jesus enjoyed kids. And kids seemed drawn to Jesus. Parents were bringing their children and asking Jesus to bless them.

James, a son of thunder, was probably one of the disciples who scolded these parents for bothering Jesus. Remember, James also wanted to call down fire from Heaven on a town because they did not welcome Jesus. So I wouldn't be surprised to hear that James was probably also zealous in guarding Jesus' time and energy. And these parents bringing their kids to be blessed... well, this just wouldn't do. Jesus had much more important things to attend to.

Jesus was angry when he realized what was happening.

"Listen!" He told His disciples. "This is what the Kingdom of God looks like—these children. Unless you can receive it like a child, you'll never be a part of it."

What could He have meant?

I'm not certain I have a complete understanding of His words. But there are a few things I have observed.

On our pilgrimage through life here on earth, we start out believing and trusting. We believe what our parents tell us. We believe what adults tell us the Bible says. We trust those things.

Until we learn to not believe.

That's right, we learn to not trust. We learn to question and doubt. We learn to put our greatest belief in what the world calls *reality* instead of learning to trust God's reality. We learn to scrutinize and analyze with our human minds the things that are of the heavenly realm. (Is there anything more foolish?)

The world teaches us, and we learn to not believe.

I thought about the chickens that jumped off the sheriff's plate in Santo Domingo. When I first heard the story, I'll be honest, my reaction was, *Well, of course people believed that. They were too ignorant to know better.*

But now I must ask myself: Are miracles possible? Doesn't Jesus say that His disciples will do even greater things than He did? Those are the words of Jesus; therefore I cannot discount them. Am I going to believe what He said? He raised a few people from the dead. Compared to that, what's a few chickens?

If I cannot believe, how can I trust in a God I cannot see? How can I keep on going in this journey, believing there is a place being prepared for me in the jasper-walled city? How can I accept that Jesus rose from the dead and so I will also live again?

Could I learn something from little children who so completely believe in those they trust?

If I cannot believe, how will I see the Kingdom of God in all its glory?

Looking back, I realize what a gift that evening was. It was a gathering of people from many cultures and life experiences who shared one common goal. We shared the road and we shared the destination. The gathering of these people around one table carved out a few hours that were a precious part of my pilgrimage.

I caught a glimpse of the gift that night. I even voiced my thoughts to Judit.

"Enjoy this night. When this hike is finished and we get home, we'll look back on this time and realize just how special this moment is. I'm telling you, I know this; I've experienced it. For some reason, when we're in the middle of something, we don't really enjoy it to the fullest. But later we look back and realize what an amazing experience we've had."

25

Life in a Ghost Town

As we left Astorga the next morning, the path began its upward ascent toward the mountains. We walked on an old asphalt highway and more trees provided shade, but there was no doubt about it—we were climbing. We would soon be at the highest point of the entire Camino.

We passed through Rabanal del Camino, a pleasant town that was the recommended stop for this day, and pushed on 5 more kilometers to a mountain village. After Rabanal, those last 5 kilometers were the steepest part of the day, and we had beautiful views over the surrounding territory. The towns we would meet on this mountain passage were almost ghost towns, populated only with crumbling buildings that looked like the ruins of some ancient civilization.

LIFE IN A GHOST TOWN

The little mountain village—if it could be called a village—of Foncebadón was reminiscent of images of hippie communes in the United States in the Sixties. Goats scrambled on crumbling walls. Old cars and trucks rested in tall grass. We passed a "residence" someone had cobbled together from the front end of a van and a small camper. The road was mostly dirt and pieces of broken stone. Many of the buildings were abandoned and falling down, with their roofs gone. Piles of rubble created a landscape of disrepair.

Still, the town seemed to be coming back to life. Only in the last decade has pilgrimage on the Camino once again become popular, and these tiny communities are now offering their assistance and aid to pilgrims. Our hostel, the Albergue Monte Irago, was a beautiful, two-story stone building.

And what luck for my vegetarian friend! The hostel served vegetarian meals. To my mind, a vegetarian meal is several pounds of rice mixed with rice, the combination of which is then enhanced with a mixture of other rice. Our pilgrim meals invariably included a salad or soup, but even those were questioned by Lori. *Is there any kind of meat in the soup?* Most of the main courses were fish or pork or chicken. Occasionally, when vegetarian choices were non-existent, Lori would eat fish, but she usually ordered paella (if it was meatless). I did try the paella one night. If you don't mind eating all that rice, it actually is a good meal.

When Lori discovered that yoga sessions were held in the barn next to the hostel, she offered to lead a class. She's quite good at yoga, and had done this before in another town. At that time, I was working on my blog and had missed the session. This time, I decided I'd drop in and see what it was all about.

The barn was dilapidated, and the roof looked like it might drop in on us at any moment. On the lower level, twelve mattresses were laid out on the floor; apparently these were used for overflow when the hostel was full. We stood on the mattresses and tried to follow Lori's instructions and example. It was impossible for me. How do you position your leg in one most unnatural way, with great discomfort extend your arm in another direction, and still keep your body from tumbling over? Balancing on one foot and one hand? Impossible.

The tall Asian dude showed up for class. This was the third time we met him. He had been at the fruit stand the day before as we walked toward Astorga. I assumed he was staying there, but here he was again. Was he a pilgrim? No one remembered seeing him on the trail.

Now he was determined to demonstrate his yoga expertise—of which there obviously was none. He tried to duplicate everything Lori did, but fell flat. He really wasn't much better at it than the skinny Mennonite from Ohio.

He was good at playing the singing bowl, though. One aid to meditation in yoga is the use of "singing" bowls, which actually make a kind of music when you rub your hand around the rim. As kids, we used to make water glasses hum by doing the same thing; filling them with different amounts of liquid produced different pitches. Our tall mystery man picked up the brass bowl and soon had it singing.

It was a day and a place unlike any other day and place on the Camino de Santiago. We were high on the mountain—almost to the highest point on the Camino—and the views were beautiful. The town itself was absolutely desolate, but the people I was with transformed the experience. Grace was there and Angelina and my new friend Judit.

By the way, it turned out that I had assumed incorrectly—Judit was not the daughter of the arrogant man who sat beside her in Astorga. They had met on the trail, as all of us had. I had also misjudged the man's character, but I would not know that until Santiago.

26

Into the Mountains

In less than two miles the next morning, we stood at the highest point on the Camino. Here, a famous cross is outlined against the sky, a simple iron cross topping a 16-foot wooden pole. This has become a symbol of the Way of Saint James and also marks what is sometimes referred to as the Gateway to the Mountains. The cross itself rises out of a huge mound of rocks.

Some historians theorize that the pile of rocks probably existed long before the cross. About a thousand years before the birth of Christ, the region from here to the sea was inhabited by the Celts, and their custom was to mark passages—especially those over mountains and high places—with piles of rocks called cairns. Today, the word and the practice are still in use. Cairns often mark the way for hikers, especially in areas with little signage. After the Celts, the Romans conquered the territory, and they followed a similar custom. Someone at some time placed a cross there, making it a Christian site. Now this cross, La Cruz de Ferro, has become a spiritually significant point for many pilgrims.

The suggested practice is that when pilgrims leave their homes, they carry with them a rock or other heavy object. Practically, it cannot be too large, but density is important—one needs to feel the weight of it in the backpack as the journey progresses. This rock symbolizes something that the pilgrim wants to leave behind, to shed, or to remove from his life. The pilgrim carries the burden along the Camino, burdened with its weight. At the cross, the rock is dropped on the huge pile already there, and the pilgrim leaves it behind—lightening both the load he carries on his back and the burden on his soul.

The rocks are often inscribed. Some are also left as memorials to loved ones or as a symbolic representation of a prayer. The pile of stones mounds up around the pole; thousands of folks have left their burdens here at the cross.

I had not carried a rock with me on this hike, but I had done a similar thing at the end of my Appalachian Trail hike as I dropped my burden of grief at the cross on the top of Mt. Katahdin in Maine.

The next mountain town was Manjarin, population 1. That's right. One person. This town is deserted except for the house—not much more than a shed—of Tomás, who is dedicated to serving pilgrims. He offers foam mattresses on the floor, an outdoor toilet, and cold showers, but there is also a special meal cooked in the evening, music, an outside fire, and an atmosphere that some pilgrims have called "magical" and "unforgettable." I cannot vouch for those endorsements. We passed by this one-building town without stopping.

I loved looking out over the mountainsides and seeing the small villages tucked into a curve of a hill or along a river valley. The views were always changing and always fantastic.

By the end of the day, though, we had descended into a fertile river valley and were in Ponferrada, a modern city of almost 70,000. Just outside the city, we toured the ruins of the magnificent Templar Castle. Its high stone walls, towers, turrets, and walkways still appear to guard the city as colorful flags fly from the watchtowers. Built in the thirteenth century with a moat and two heavy gates, it was a stronghold of the Templar Knights who had organized to protect pilgrims traveling to holy places. By the time this castle was built, the Knights Templars had become a rich and powerful force in Europe, so much so that in the next century the French king, fearing their power, began a campaign to discredit members of the order. Their power and organization quickly declined as they were accused of heresy and subterfuge and were thus arrested and executed.

It was really too bad that the knights were no longer around. Lori was making plans that might require their knightly protection.

Ahead of us lay another choice. At the border of Galicia, we would be faced with the steepest climb of our hike. There, as on the very first day when we left St. Jean, we would have a choice of routes. The easiest, shortest route follows the main highway. Most pilgrims take this path. A second, more scenic route, requires a steeper climb and is longer. The third option is remote and dangerous. The guidebook has stern cautionary warnings. *For experienced walkers only. Don't walk this route if you lack confidence or in poor weather... Take food with you... the only bar is often closed... Waymarking is poor so you need a good sense of direction and reserve energy to retrace your steps should you get lost.*

Of course, this more strenuous and dangerous route is supposedly also the most spectacular. And of course Lori wanted to hike this third route, named the *Camino Dragonte*.

The previous day in Foncebadón, Lori had already started campaigning, trying to find someone who would agree to hike the Camino Dragonte with her. I had declined, offering instead to go Route Number Two, the more moderate one over the mountain. She wanted *spectacular*, though, so she had been polling the other modern Knights Templars (read, men protectors) in her search.

There was a chance a knight just might come along and grant Lori's wish. Some of them were enchanted with her charm and good looks and might actually accompany her on the misadventure. This was of some concern to me, simply because if Lori left my company then so did my phone charger. *Her* phone charger, to be more accurate. I had sent mine ahead in that package to Santiago when we lightened our load, and I was now sharing hers. So that day in Ponferrada, I stopped in a store and bought a charger for myself, just in case.

That day I also began to adjust my mistake. The tall man who had first joined us at supper in Astorga and whom I had immediately slapped with a label (*arrogant and cocky*, you will remember), picked up a guitar in the hostel dining room that evening and led everyone in singing "La Bomba." The more I saw of this man, the more I thought that perhaps my initial judgment might have been too hasty.

Our hostel in Ponferrada, San Nicolás de Flüe, was large, modern, and comfortable, with 200 beds but only four to a room. We had arrived at the hostel early, before they were open for check-in. Other pilgrims were there too, and everyone milled around the courtyard outside. Someone had a brilliant idea: Let's soak our feet in the fountain. That luxury didn't last long—an authoritative person came out and informed us that no feet were to enter the soothing waters. So we put our shoes back on and stood in line, waiting.

It's difficult to be patient when the most important thing is to get inside and head for the showers to clean up. Word passed among the pilgrims that showers and a laundry were available at a nearby church, and some left to seek out those accommodations.

Finally, three volunteers came out and started the check-in process. The line moved slowly. At last Lori and I stood in front of the table—and then a commotion erupted in the crowd, and everything stopped once again.

One exhausted pilgrim had fainted and fallen head first into the waters of the fountain. The folks checking us in stopped to see what the commotion was about and what they would have to do about it. But several other pilgrims had already dragged out the dripping one, and he revived quickly.

Can we please just get back to business? I need a shower.

27

Little Santiago

The Meseta was already forgotten. Between Ponferrada and Villafranca, the terrain of hills and vineyards was rich with many shades of green and the vibrancy refreshed me. The scenes reminded me of Greece. No, I've never been there, but this was what I imagine Greece looks like.

Towns clung to the hillsides, and in almost all of them we spotted more of the stork nests high on electric poles or church steeples. I had first seen these nests along the route through the Meseta, and now they were commonplace.

Many times our path was on dirt or gravel lanes, winding through the vineyards, with the mountains always lining the horizon. Actually, the hills were turning into mountains. Some of the vineyards were planted in artistic terraces on steep slopes. This fertile wine country of the river valley is known as

Bierzo, and the modern yet picturesque town of Villafranca is also a tourist destination with shops and restaurants and, of course, local wines.

In addition to being a tourist town, Villafranca is also sometimes called "little Santiago." Its importance to pilgrims lies in the opportunity to end a pilgrimage here if absolutely necessary. The Villafranca church, dedicated to St. James, has an impressive northern entrance called the "Door of Forgiveness." If a pilgrim was too sick or weak to continue, he could receive here the communion and forgiveness of sins and perhaps the healing or miracle he had hoped to find in Santiago.

Lori and I asked for recommendations of a good restaurant, and we were directed to an old establishment that offered views out over the river. The place was beautiful and had an aura of homeyness. I immediately noticed the family at one table who was having fun, laughing, and enjoying themselves. This was a comfortable, pleasant place, and I settled into my chair, ready to enjoy the evening.

Lori asked about vegetarian options. The best they could do for her was a fish entrée, and she settled for that. I ordered the same.

Our meals came out and the plates were set before us.

Lori took one look, gasped, and recoiled in horror. There were two fish lying on her plate, body and head still intact.

The fish we had been served at previous restaurants was always a filet. Lori had been totally unprepared for those dead eyes staring up at her. She was aghast, leaning back, away from the plate.

"They're looking at me!" It was a wail of distress.

Since I had just had my armor brilliantly polished on the previous day at the castle, I rescued the damsel in distress.

"Do you want me to cut the heads off?"

She pushed the plate across the table, and I dispatched those heads quickly, moving them to my plate. Now four fish heads stared up at me.

I sent two bodies back over to Lori, and she managed to go on with her meal.

With my two fish, I had a rich, brothy soup. The broth was delicious, but there were dark things floating around in it that I could not quite evaluate. I ate it, though, and was almost finished when Lori looked at me with a smile and asked, "How was the blood sausage?"

Now it was my turn to recoil in horror. I pushed the dish away and did not finish the soup.

We had lost one of the pilgrims in our group. A few days before, Zoe had parted from our company, taking a different route because she had plans to fly home and needed to be in Santiago a day or two before we would arrive.

Grace had stayed with us, but here in Villafranca, she decided she needed a break from hostel life and checked into the Parador.

We added another face, though, when we met Debbie, a young lady from Canada. She had started the Camino ten days after we had left St. Jean, yet now she had caught up with us. How had she done that? In answer to my query, she said she hiked fast because there was nothing to see and she was bored.

Our hostel that night was a small, private establishment called Albergue de la Piedra. It's built against the rock wall of a steep hill, and part of the rock juts into the dining room, incorporated into the design of the building. My guidebook offers a number of lodging options in Villafranca but warns, *Wherever you stay make sure you get a good night's sleep to fortify yourself for the strenuous but stupendous hike the next day. Tomorrow brings us up and over the pass into O'Cebreiro and Galicia.*

28

Over the Pass

The path to Galicia threaded between two buildings and immediately started climbing a steep incline. At least, that was the start of our path the next morning.

Lori and I took the second of the three choices over the next mountain—a road that was the longest of the three but at least did not present the danger of the Camino Dragonte. Everyone who had been invited to join Lori on her march to her possible demise had declined, and thus she had settled for a compromise with me.

Most of the folks staying at our hostel had chosen the easiest route, following the road. If it had not been for Lori's insistence, I probably would have stayed with the group. As it turned out, this was a beautiful hike and I was happy we had made this choice. I was also happy that, although it was a strenuous climb, it did offer the possibility of arriving safely at the end of the day.

We walked through groves of chestnut trees as we ascended and enjoyed the views out over the Valcarce Valley. We watched the sunrise from atop the mountain and caught glimpses of the road snaking through the valley far below. There were no other pilgrims in sight, and we met no one. We passed a large garden, evidence that there was life somewhere nearby, but most of the walk was as solitary as the occasional abandoned buildings where weeds and moss crept over the walls.

Coming down off the mountain, we rejoined the main route following the highway and took a break at a major truck stop at La Portela de Valcarce. Sometimes sections of the Camino that closely followed busy roads are actually more dangerous than remote and steep mountain passages. The highways, it seems, give no consideration to the safety of pilgrims. At times we did not even have crosswalks or bridges to cross the highway safely—it was a matter of darting across whenever there was a break in traffic.

The Dragon route descended to join us again in the riverside town of Herrerías. Something about this small town called out to me and encouraged me to slow down and observe all the life happening here.

By "life" I mean the simple acts of our daily existence. An old man leaned on his cane as he worked his way down the rows of his garden, sending a gentle rain from a watering can to small green plants. He was oblivious to the pilgrim who watched him. A barber shop door hung ajar, and I passed slowly, snatching a glimpse of the barber in animated conversation with a patron in the chair. Several ladies bustled about, sweeping their sidewalks. Front doors stood open, allowing sunshine to illuminate homey scenes. Two men were splitting wood and piling it in a wheelbarrow. I met a lady coming out of the post office. Lapsing into that universal language of hand motions and smiles, I expressed my desire to take her picture. She posed, her face beaming.

These scenes were framed by colorful flowers planted along the roadway, on top of a stone fence, and in window boxes. I walked through Herrerías and savored these little snippets of life in a small town.

For whatever reason that day, in this town, I was acutely aware of the beauty of living. Most of the time, we are so busy existing that we miss the beauty.

The guidebook's few paragraphs about Herrerías include this advice: *Fill up the water flask and gird your loins for the final assault on the mountain ahead.*

The flask was watered and loins were girded as we headed out of town and went up and up... and still up. O'Cebreiro is more than 2600 feet higher than Villafranca, where we had started that morning. Nearing the top of the mountain, we passed a stone marker that told us we were entering Galicia, the final third of our Camino pilgrimage. From this point on, at every half kilometer a marker notes the distance to Santiago.

Often these markers are adorned with carvings of Camino symbols and also announce the name of the town or village we are entering. Just one kilometer later, we passed the marker proclaiming that we were in O'Cebreiro and it was 151 kilometers to Santiago, a little less than 94 more miles.

The views were amazing. We could see for miles, looking out over the mountains and their patchwork of green fields and forests interspersed with small hamlets, all stitched together with the winding highways and country lanes.

For most of the day, the sky above was a cloudless blue; occasionally huge, billowing gray clouds filled the heavens and cast their shadows over the landscapes. I remembered that Galicia is known for its rapid changes in weather. Its mountains capture the moisture carried from the Atlantic Ocean. There was a small umbrella at the bottom of my backpack, but I did not need it that day. The dark clouds passed, and the sky was blue again.

O'Cebreiro is a town of stone atop the mountain. Streets and fences and buildings are all stone, of various hues and shapes. Here we began to see the traditional pallozas, circular stone buildings with conical, thatched roofs that were once commonly used as dwellings. Many are now vacation homes or museums.

This was the mountaintop town we had heard about, where the albergue has open showers with no doors. No thank you. We chose accommodations elsewhere.

On my way to meet Grace and Lori for supper, I caught sight of Teresa sitting by herself on a stone wall. Our paths had crossed several times on the Camino; we would see her in the towns, but she stayed in private hotels or inns. Now I noticed she was crying.

Her husband of 36 years had died three years before. They had had a good marriage and were very much in love, and his death devastated Teresa. She felt as though her life was over. I asked her if the trail was wearing her down.

No, she replied through her sniffles. This hike was saving her life. I could understand that. I had experienced the same thing on the Appalachian Trail.

Yet she was still grieving deeply, terribly lonely without her best friend. Her life, she remarked, was much like the piles the cows left behind on the lanes we traveled. (She used a different word, though.)

I asked her what made her happy. What brought her joy? She thought awhile and remarked that this trail, the views, and the beauty brought her joy. Her sisters and family brought her joy. Gradually her tears dried as she recounted other good things in her life.

This conversation with Teresa would come back to me throughout the next day and stay with me a long time. We were within days of the eighth anniversary of my wife's death, and of course this prompted me to ponder once again my great loss and how it had changed my life. But I also listed for myself all the good still in my life: my children and grandchildren, my parents and sisters and brothers-in-law, my friends, my church, my material blessings, and my work—work that includes having great adventures and opening my life to share with others.

Teresa could not know it, but that conversation may have benefitted me more than it did her.

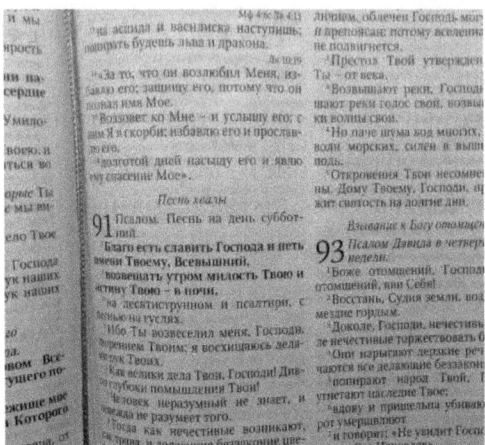

29

91, Again

Outside the stone church in O'Cebreiro is a bust of Don Elias Valiña Sampedro who was a priest here for thirty years in the last half of the twentieth century. If it were not for him, I might very well have never walked the Camino de Santiago.

Sampedro had studied and written about the Camino pilgrimage, but when he attempted to walk the French Camino himself, he found that many of the old paths and trails had almost been lost. He made it his mission to save this path, and he was the person responsible for painting all the yellow arrows that marked our way. He also organized groups to maintain the trails. The pilgrimage that was such an important route in medieval times had almost been forgotten, but in the last 25 years since his work, hundreds of thousands of pilgrims have walked to Santiago.

But it was inside the stone church that I came upon something that meant even more to me.

Let's go back twelve years. We had just received the devastating news from Mary's surgeon that surgery had gone well, but the cancer had spread. She had several months to several years to live.

Seated on her hospital bed, I opened my Bible at random and read Psalm 91, those comforting verses about dwelling in the shelter of the Most High and resting in the shadow of the Almighty.

Verse 14 promised that God would protect those who love Him and would honor them with long life. Mary claimed that promise and the entire psalm as her own. She read it every day for the four years she had left on this earth. The message at her funeral service was taken from Psalm 91.

In those years, I made a habit of reading through the Bible twice a year. I continued after Mary's death, and on my first day on the Appalachian Trail, the next chapter of my reading "just happened" to be Psalm 91.

There I was, setting off on a five-month trek from Georgia to Maine, sleeping in the wilderness in either a tent or a shelter. And on that uncertain and fearful first day, I read the promise in Psalm 91: While sleeping in an earthly shelter, I would also be dwelling in the shelter of the Most High, and no disaster would come near my tent. How's that for reassurance when starting down an unknown path with no idea of what awaited me?

For many, this "coincidence" would have meant nothing. For me, it meant the world. I had learned to look for signs from God that were intended for me. How often do we miss these, or, even if we do see them, we discount them as "coincidence" and meaningless?

There were more Psalm 91 reassurances still to come.

Approximately 2,000 folks a year attempt a thru-hike of the AT. Only ten to fifteen percent actually achieve it. The folks of the AT conference try to determine how many actually finish by conducting several check points.

At the beginning of the hike in Georgia, I signed my name and trail name, "Apostle," and registered as hiker 391 beginning the hike. Halfway through my hike, I stopped at the AT headquarters in Harpers Ferry to sign in. There I was hiker 191. I had passed or outlasted 200 other hikers. Not bad for an aging hiker, I thought. The day finally arrived when I hiked into Baxter State Park in Maine and prepared for my final day on the trail. At a ranger station, I checked in for the final time. I again signed my trail name in the official book of completed hikes. "Apostle, Georgia-Maine, 2008." I was hiker number 91 finishing the trail.

The number 91 had followed me the entire way. It was as if God was telling me that everything was okay, and I was right where He had planned for me to be. I felt God saying, *All is well. Go finish the hike, then do what I told you to do.*

On the Camino, I did not visit all the cathedrals and churches along the way as some pilgrims do. But on the mountaintop in O'Cebreiro, I felt compelled to enter the stone church. On a wall inside, a glass display case held several dozen open Bibles. Each Bible was from a different country, in a different language, and tagged with the name of the country.

In the middle of the display, one particular Bible caught my attention. The Russian Bible was opened to Psalm 91.

There it was—a message from God to me. I was a stranger in a foreign land, yet I felt God telling me I was right where He wanted me to be. Peace filled me, the same peace I had received that day when I realized I was hiker 91 ascending Mount Katahdin in Maine. *All is well; you're right where you're supposed to be.*

God speaks to His people in many ways. Watch for His messages. Listen for His voice.

30

Galicia

Less than twenty-four hours had passed since I had entered Galicia, and I already knew that I loved this section of Spain. The next few days confirmed it. Like the Basque area, Galicia has its own language and distinctive culture and is very independent. Names are even spelled differently here than in other areas of Spain.

Temperatures are moderate, even chilly on the mountains; and forests and fields are green and vibrant. It's a rainy, misty land, although we experienced less rain than expected. Our path was often along country lanes and old paths that have borne many footsteps. Stone walls line the trail on steep hillsides, small hamlets huddle in the dells or hang on the hillsides and offer pilgrims a friendly and generous welcome. The menus were increasingly built around seafood. We were, after all, nearing the ocean and the end of the earth.

The culture and the spirit of Galicia hold many lingering influences of the Celtic people. Some of those influences are decidedly from an ancient pagan past, long before Christ arrived in this world as a human. Spirituality is tied more closely to the earth and the mystical element is stronger here than anywhere else I've been. Many names of places refer to ancient Celtic deities; witchcraft is still active here; and pagan legends and myths endure.

Is this why James the Apostle was sent to Galicia? We have no way of knowing, but God does place people where He needs them. Perhaps the spiritual awareness of the people made them more receptive than some cultures to Christianity—there are many, many monasteries in Galicia and the stone crosses that appear everywhere in towns and along the roads have become a symbol of this area. Like each one of us, Galicia has come to be what it is today as a result of its spiritual history.

Enough of the geography and history. Let me also tell you that one of the things I found charming in the little villages was the cow piles. Yes, they really do bring the cows home through the streets. At times we were compelled to step aside and wait while the herd passed. Barns are often set right along main street, and I frequently walked by open barn doors and enjoyed pungent reminders of my own community back home.

We left O'Cebreiro by the light of our headlamps. Three narrow shafts of light bobbed and wove through the thick fog as we carefully followed the path out of town. Another pilgrim was stumbling through the misty darkness with no illumination. We sandwiched her between us and proceeded single file down the narrow shoulder of the highway.

Slowly the sun made its appearance and from the fog emerged beautiful views of the countryside. Wispy mists lingered a bit longer in the valleys below us and sometimes made islands out of hilltops.

We were in farm country, and we met many big dogs—German Shepherds and other intimidating breeds. But most of them greeted us with wagging tails. They are so accustomed to strangers passing through that they don't even bother barking.

Triacastela had been our planned stopping point for the day, but several encounters with hikers during the day changed our plans. A retired heart surgeon from the United States had fallen in with us for a short while. He remarked that he was planning to visit an ancient monastery in Samos, one of the oldest and largest in the western world. The history of this monastery sounded interesting, and since we all believed we would never again have the chance to visit, we agreed to detour toward Samos.

It would be a long day of walking. Then we learned from another hiker that halfway to Samos was a recently remodeled monastery that was open to pilgrims. The remodeling had been extensive and elaborate, costing two million euros. That sounded like an acceptable place to lay our heads. We decided to stop there and walk on to the Samos monastery in the morning.

It was a quiet and tranquil walk. The three of us were the only hikers to advance beyond Triacastela. We also were the only three to arrive at the remodeled monastery.

When we arrived at the hostel—quite isolated and off the beaten path—a lonely fellow sat outside lamenting his bad fortune. He was very disgruntled, miserable, and bit up. The place he had stayed the night before had bedbugs and now he was looking for facilities to wash his belongings and get cleaned up.

I had not been concerned about bedbugs up to this point. We had read warnings about the pestilence, but most places change bedding every day and give pilgrims a sheet liner and pillow liner to use—which is then thrown away the next day. We'd heard, too, that the bugs are more apt to be in beds along the outer walls of a building, and so we usually tried to stay away from those bunks. If a place is found to be infested, everything is removed and sterilized. Most places take great care to prevent these problems, but we did hear of some bedbug incidents.

After listening to this pilgrim's story, I always checked my mattress.

There were plenty of choices of beds that night in this new, upscale hostel. In a 60-bed establishment, we were the only three guests. Three of us, in a massive, multi-million-euro facility. The place was eerie; it needed people.

31

A Little Rain

We arrived in Samos the next morning at 8:00am. The great monastery lay below our path, and as we approached, we had a birds-eye view of what looked like a castle awaiting us in the morning mists.

The monastery would not open for tours until 9:00am. We went across the street for breakfast and an extended coffee hour to wait for the tour.

It was worth the wait. The monastery is an impressive place, but I was particularly fascinated with the collection of art. We also had a glimpse of the hostel where we had planned to stay before making the choice for the remodeled monastery. It was a bleak room with twenty or thirty beds in one area. I decided the eerie, empty monastery-turned-mansion was slightly more comfortable than this place would have been.

Our intended stop that night was Sarria, but it was a bit too crowded, so we moved on.

Sarria is crowded with pilgrims for a reason. This city is 112 kilometers from Santiago, and any pilgrim starting here and arriving at the cathedral in Santiago—walking at least 100 kilometers, in other words—is qualified to receive a compostela.

Some folks will start their Camino here because of physical limitations that prevent their walking a longer route; others walk this shorter route because they want only one thing—the compostela, which is a respected document when job seeking; and still others seem to have come only for a bit of fun.

It is that group seeking only fun that it is most difficult to be patient with. They sometimes travel by taxi over difficult stretches; they travel in groups that always stay together and do not mix well on the trail; and they just generally create a commotion and detract from the solemnity of pilgrimage. Some have called them "pseudo-pilgrims," but we long-distance pilgrims are encouraged to be nice to them anyway.

When I reached Santiago, I noticed a marked difference between pilgrims. Those who had only walked 100 kilometers were the loudest and most boisterous after finishing the Camino. The rest of us who had hiked the entire Camino finished with a quiet confidence instilled by mountains climbed, plains traversed, and acquaintances made and cherished.

We were in town when two buses arrived and a massive crowd of people descended and swarmed at us. Too crowded. We moved on.

Four kilometers past Sarria, we found the Albergue Pombal in Barbadelo. The place had twelve beds—and not much else.

In a tiny store, Grace and Lori purchased the ingredients for a spaghetti meal which they cooked in a small kitchen area. I did my part in the meal preparation by staying out of the way.

Our detour to the monastery at Samos and now this extended walk past Sarria meant we were separating ourselves from many of the folks we had been hiking with. But it also meant we had gained a day on Zoe, who was somewhere ahead of us.

Another frequent sight throughout the Galician countryside are the small buildings, often on stilts or stone pillars, with slatted wooden walls and pitched roofs. Many are similar in size to the backyard storage barns or garden sheds so popular in Amish Country today. Most of these small structures were empty, and Lori and I debated their purpose.

My dear vegetable-eater insisted that since we were in an area known for witchcraft, this must be some sort of "spirit house." Nearly every home had one, she reasoned; it was probably something associated with the Celtic deities.

I laughed heartily at this wild idea and pointed out to her that any spirit within could easily escape through the gaps in the wall.

One day we passed one of these *horreos* and the door was standing open. We peered inside, to see ears of corn.

"You see, Lori, they're grain bins used to dry grain. They're up on stilts to keep the grain out of reach of rats and mice."

She had a reply for that. The corn, she thought, could possibly be food for the resident spirits to nibble on.

Only when informed by a local resident that I was indeed correct did she relent and admit that she was wrong... or I was right. Both were equally hard for her to concede.

The next day we had an early start and arrived in Portomarín, our next scheduled stop, in early afternoon, crossing a long bridge and then walking up a flight of stairs to the town square. It was Sunday, and the cathedral had emptied. It was also raining steadily, the first real downpour we had had on the entire Camino.

We found a table outside a café and had ice cream on the covered porch. Grace, who had kept in touch with Zoe since they had separated, was checking the guidebook and calculating. When she realized her niece was only 13 kilometers ahead of us, she took out her umbrella and determined to go on hiking and reunite with Zoe so they could walk the final miles into Santiago together.

We said our goodbyes, but I noticed the longing look on Lori's face as she watched Grace disappear down the street. She and Zoe had bonded and walked together most of the time; she was missing her friend. Now Grace was also moving ahead, and Lori experienced another loss. I knew what was coming, even before she spoke.

Lori wanted to keep walking and catch up with her friends. *Oh, no, no, no. I do not want to walk in this rain.*

All I wanted to do was find a room at an albergue. I had not brought my rain gear to Spain. Do not ask me why I neglected that. I was so miserable in countless days of rain on the AT that I was certain mushrooms were going to sprout on my body. I hated walking in the rain. So why had I brought only a small umbrella for this hike? I have no answer for that.

I had just convinced Lori of the folly of hiking on in the rain when she gave a shout of glee. There was Grace, coming back toward us. She had forgotten her hiking sticks.

Lori and Grace grabbed each other as if they'd been separated for years and Lori started to cry. I knew my plans were done, washed away by Lori's tears. I dug out my own small umbrella.

I couldn't believe I was going to walk out into the pouring rain. Here we were in town, ready to take refuge and stay dry and be well-fed and rested—instead, the distress of a fair maiden was prompting me to abandon comfort and do that very thing I detest.

When I nodded yes to Lori, she had her rain gear on in record time. Mine was still at home in a closet.

Up went my umbrella and away we went. I decided the rain was not going to ruin my day and I tried singing all the songs about rain that I could remember. The umbrella, however, did ruin my hiking rhythm. Two hiking sticks and one umbrella. How does one hold three instruments with only two hands? I started out holding the umbrella in one hand and both sticks in the other. Finally I shoved the umbrella into the strap on my backpack, and that held it in place for a while, although in reality the refuge it offered was pitiful.

Thirteen kilometers later, we found Zoe at a pleasant albergue and the women had a joyful reunion. I was soaking wet and only wanted to dry out. The hostel had beds for us; we checked in; and after a hot shower and a change to dry clothes, I was also joyful.

The long day ended with a satisfying meal at a small restaurant.

The fact is, if you're a pilgrim you're going to be walking in some rain. You can choose to wallow in the misery of it or you can sing your way through Plan B, even though your umbrella is too small and your shoes are squishing with every step.

32

Santiago in Sight

The choice to push on that day (even though I didn't think it was a choice at the time) would affect the rest of our Camino in regards to who we would meet and what would happen in our remaining days.

We had gained an entire day, moving our expected arrival in Santiago up one more day. Although we had hiked away from our "bubble" of pilgrims, we now had opportunities to meet new hikers. One day ahead of us and one day behind us, there were other bubbles, communities of hikers who had bonded as family from their days together on the trail. We, though, were now one of the lost tribes of Israel, wandering along on our own.

Fortunately, even though we were a day ahead of our bubble, we would have an extra day to wait in Santiago and see our tribe arrive at the finish line.

The downpour was over by morning, and it was a beautiful day to hike. We left town just as dawn was breaking. I was certain I heard it break.

Fog hovered over the landscape. Fields of sunflowers and wheat had changed to fields of corn. The agricultural area felt familiar to me; I recognized many of the crops in fields and gardens.

I did not recognize what lay before me on the plate. Well, I knew what it was. But I had never before seen *pulpo Gallega*.

Nor had I eaten this local delicacy, the octopus of Galicia.

But today was the day.

We had stopped at a café in Melide. Directly inside the main entrance, the chef executioner stood behind a counter, snipping bits of octopus into manageable servings. Behind him on a burner was a boiling, steaming kettle where the eight-legged sea creature was being cooked.

We seated ourselves in the busy dining room and pretended to enjoy our octopus. It's an acquired taste that I did not acquire that day, and never will. That was the one and only day I will eat octopus.

And that's about all I can say about that.

Pilgrims coming from another Camino route beginning on the north coast of Spain join the main route to Santiago in Melide. Everything was becoming busier—the path, the hostels, even the cafés in the little villages. I tried to imagine the lines of pilgrims weaving their way over the countryside behind me and ahead of me. The organization of American Pilgrims on the Camino reports that the records of the Pilgrims' Welcome Office in Santiago show 237,886 pilgrims received a compostela in 2014. And remember, there are many, many people like Aoife who walk only part of the Camino, never intending to reach Santiago.

After we left Melide, the route led over delightful stone bridges and through tunnels of trees pressing up against the pathway.

We ended our day in a small town called Boente, staying at the Os Albergue. Directly across the street was a church where a parish priest is normally available to bless passing pilgrims and stamp their credentials. For some reason, the priest was not there when I arrived, but a small table with ink pad and stamp was set up for any pilgrim to self-stamp. I waited to do so. The wait was due not to a line of pilgrims but to one young man who carried in a stack of at least a dozen credentials and stamped each one.

I strolled along the back streets, observing life in this small town. There were mainly old folks here. One old man pushed a wheelbarrow with freshly picked produce. A curious puppy jumped on a stone wall and followed alongside me for a bit. A black flower presented itself to match my mood.

Only two days remained in my Camino journey, and a sort of melancholy was settling over me. I had fashioned a new reality here in Spain, and now the fact that my new reality would soon end was beginning to bother me. I hate endings.

And now another ending loomed in my life.

With every marker we passed, counting down the distance to Santiago de Compostela, I mourned a bit. I had felt the same way on the day I finally came within sight of the sign marking the end of the Appalachian Trail on top of Mt. Katahdin. That trek had taken me through snow and freezing rain, suffocating heat, dangerous river crossings, a tornado, physical and emotional exhaustion, and terrible loneliness—and finally it was all finished. Should I not be exultant?

But the ironic twist is that when a dream has finally become a reality, it is no longer a dream. No matter how wonderful the accomplishment, we also have in some ways experienced a loss. It is over. The dream is done. What now?

The feelings that hounded me all day were familiar; nevertheless, they were also unsettling.

We left Boente before daylight, but there was no need to turn on our headlamps. A beautiful full moon hung low in the western sky, softening the harshness of daytime details with its gentle light. Homes lay sleeping in the ethereal light, and we walked in an enchanted landscape.

I hiked by myself. The end was near. Every fiber in my body felt it. My body was actually in much better shape than when I had started the Camino. As for my mind and spirit—well, that remained to be seen. I wasn't quite sure what the state of my mind and spirit were now that Santiago was just ahead.

We stopped in Arca, 12.5 miles from our final destination. We had entered the outer belt of urban sprawl I know so well from cities in the States. The town seemed to consist primarily of gas stations, restaurants, pharmacies, and other such businesses. Somehow, this was not right. The last night of my Camino should have been in a remote and contemplative spot on a mountainside or in the middle of a plain under the vast heavens. Yes, it should have been in a field of stars.

We met many new faces at Albergue Edreira since our bubble was a day behind us.

I spent considerable time walking around town alone while contemplating all that had happened on this hike. As I said before, the Camino de Santiago is not so much about the physical adventure as it is about the spiritual and emotional transformations that take place. How would my life be different as a result of this hike?

That was a personal reconnaissance of sorts. A geographic reconnaissance was also necessary. We had wandered in confusion trying to find our albergue that day, so I wanted to know exactly where we would pick up the Camino to leave town the next morning. We planned to start out once again in the darkness, making it possible to arrive in Santiago early enough to get our compostelas and then be able to go to the noon mass at the cathedral, where we hoped to see the famed *Botafumeiro*.

33

Compostela

Aircraft engines roared through the darkness. Before daylight, we had already reached the edges of Santiago and skirted the back portion of the airport. It was unsettling to think that in a few days I would be back at the entrance to this airport, again in darkness, ready to board a plane to fly home.

The ending of each journey is unique. I imagine that our feelings as we close a journey are determined by what we have experienced on the pilgrimage.

The end of my Appalachian Trail hike was flooded with emotion because of both the physical and emotional difficulties I'd struggled through and also the sweetness of healing I had found. The ending of my bike ride was exciting because I had accomplished a goal; it was simply an adventure coming to an end. The Mississippi River adventure had come to an abrupt and unexpected end—and was a relief and an astounding miracle of God.

What would I feel as I walked the last kilometer of my Camino and finally held that compostela in my hand?

Daylight came, and as the road sloped gently downward, we saw Santiago awaiting us. A rainbow arched through the gray clouds and dropped into the city.

Santiago was a maze of streets. Following the yellow arrows became difficult in the sprawling, busy city. While looking for Camino symbols, we also had to keep alert and watch the traffic. Crowds of pedestrians—tourists and those going about their day-to-day business—added to our confusion.

The tall, dark-complexioned gentleman whom I had judged as a bit arrogant came striding by. An old man with a walking stick kept pace with him. I had never seen the old man before, but he barked out instructions on where to turn. He knew where the cathedral was, it seemed, and the tall dark man invited us to follow them.

Thus we marched through Santiago and entered the old section, crossing street after street. Who was this stranger we followed so blindly? Did he really know where he was going? It did not seem that he was following the yellow arrows; he knew exactly what route he wanted to follow, and he kept saying, "Follow me! Follow me! Follow me!"

We caught sight of the cathedral's spires rising above the surrounding buildings. That is, we saw a depiction of the spires. The actual structures themselves were encased in scaffolding and plastic which displayed an illustration of the spires. Renovations were under way, but pilgrims still had the sense of finally catching that glimpse of Saint Iago's great cathedral.

We heard the music, faintly at first, above the noise of the shops and the crowds. As we walked on, it became more distinct, louder, drawing us toward the Plaza de Obradoiro, the "golden" square, surrounding the cathedral. Through an arched walkway in an old wall we went, welcomed by the music of bagpipes, down a flight of stone stairs, and the plaza opened in front of us.

This entrance through the old wall is called the Gate of the Way, and musicians of some kind always welcome pilgrims as they walk through to the Plaza. During the time I was in Santiago, I also heard drums and opera singers at that spot on the stairs. It's a celebratory welcome to the city of Santiago de Compostela.

I was promised a compostela if I arrived here. Am I really ready to receive it? Am I ready to finish this pilgrimage?

So many thoughts flew through my head as I walked down those ancient stairs. Walking through the Meseta. The same thing, day after day. Then the strenuous climbs of the mountains. The feeling on some days that I just wanted to be done and go home...

And all of a sudden, I'm in the city and this pilgrimage is going to be done.

We were in the plaza, a huge courtyard, with both tourists and pilgrims milling about. Our group was still together—Lori,

Zoe, Grace, the tall dark man, and the old man who had guided us here.

We surveyed the plaza and the crowd. We had no idea what to do next. The mysterious old man pointed to one corner of the square and told us precisely where to find the Pilgrim Office, which issues the compostelas. Then he walked away from us and disappeared in the crowd. We never saw him again.

A long line of pilgrims had already formed outside the office, and we took our places at the end of the line. Even with our early start that morning, we had not arrived early enough. It was close to 10:30am. To get seats in the cathedral for the noon mass, we'd been advised to be there by 11:00am. One look at the long line ahead of us, and we knew there was no possibility of going to mass. And there was another deterrent. For security reasons, backpacks are no longer permitted in the cathedral. We would have to wait to attend mass until the next day, when we could be there early and would have stowed our backpacks at a hotel or hostel.

A man approached the back of the long line and inquired if there was any group in line. I assumed he meant a bus group, but I flippantly offered that I had a group of four. No, make that five—tall dark man was still with us.

He pulled us out of the line and informed us he would expedite our compostelas. We were all asked to fill out a form. Where had we started? (We had all started in France in St. Jean.) Why were we on the Camino? For religious or spiritual reasons, or for secular reasons, such as a vacation? There were also a few requests for personal data, one question asking for *occupation*.

The man took our completed forms and stepped into an adjacent building. When he returned, he handed us our prized compostelas. Then he turned to the tall dark man and asked excitedly, "So you're a priest?"

Imagine my surprise to hear that.

I had judged the man wrongly, from the first hour I met him. Yes, he informed us, he was a priest from Los Angeles, California. "Why didn't anyone know this?" we asked him. He had wished to remain anonymous and hike as any other pilgrim.

The man who had processed our compostelas also gave us information on how to find a tourist office where, for a few euros, we could stash our backpacks during the mass.

We arrived in the cathedral at 11:00am and found seats. Good seats.

The cathedral was packed and hundreds of folks did not get seats but stood for the entire time. I imagine that tourists and pilgrims have many different reasons for attending this service. Many, of course, are there for spiritual reasons, but just as many are probably there to witness a tradition of this pilgrim mass at the end of the journey—the swinging of the huge Botafumeiro, an incense burner suspended from the dome of the ceiling and swung back and forth over the crowd.

The mass was in Spanish, as usual, and although I did not understand the words I recognized the melody of *Ave Maria*, sung by a woman with a beautiful voice that carried throughout the huge cathedral. I sat there marveling at the sound, the crowd, and the cathedral.

A priest came up the aisle carrying a bucket of glowing embers. Attendants lifted the top off the silver Botafumeiro and dumped the embers into it. Then the huge incense burner, more than 5 feet high, was slowly raised by a rope on a pulley system high in the dome of the cathedral. Six men pulled on the other end of the rope as it slowly began to swing, then took increasingly longer sweeps, faster and faster, whooshing above our heads and spreading the incense over the crowd. It is thought that this tradition started as a way to disinfect the cathedral of whatever the pilgrims had brought in from the trail. And perhaps it was necessary to cleanse some of the smell of the pilgrims, too.

There are other rituals and traditions begun by pilgrims a thousand years ago and still followed by today's pilgrims when they arrive in Santiago. I had little knowledge of most of those. Nevertheless, I was amazed at the centuries of history here. I thought about the hundreds of thousands of pilgrims who had braved dangers and even death to finally arrive here in Santiago to have their sins forgiven or to plead in prayer for a miracle.

There was one more celebration I strongly desired to participate in—the celebration of the Eucharist. This would probably be my last chance. My longing to do so was no longer a defiant wish to do something I'd been told I could not do— no, this was a deep wish to celebrate and remember my own sins forgiven by a Savior who died for me.

Then the announcement came. Again. Those who are not practicing Catholics should not take part...where had I heard that before? Oh, everywhere.

For a second, I considered partaking anyway. I frequently have no hesitation pushing the boundaries during my travels and adventures. However, the Eucharist is a deeply spiritual thing, and I did not want to act in disrespect. I remained seated while hundreds filed forward to receive the sacraments.

But I was saddened.

Part of the afternoon was taken up with trying to find a place to stay. A few days before, another pilgrim had highly recommended a hostel supposedly in the vicinity of the cathedral, but when we asked directions we were sent to a place on a hill at the edge of town. Both Lori and I felt uneasy about this choice, but we checked in anyway. Upon further consideration, we checked out again. The place was drab, and too far from the activities and our friends who would be arriving soon.

We did find rooms at a hostel called The Last Stamp, a pleasant facility located in the midst of tourist activities and close to the cathedral.

Our friends were coming into town, some later that afternoon and some on the next day. For the remainder of this day and the next, we drifted about the cathedral's plaza and the streets and squares of old Santiago, greeting other pilgrims, sharing meals and stories, taking many pictures of each other, and savoring our last time together. Teresa came to The Last Stamp with sewing kit in hand and stitched my great North Face pants one last time. The joy of arriving in Santiago and reuniting with these friends was tempered by the knowledge that I would never see most of them again.

After a bit of research, we located the hostel that we had originally wanted to find; it was just off the square, in sight of the cathedral. Because we had already settled into The Last Stamp, we made reservations for later in the week when we would return to this city—after walking to the end of the earth.

34

To the End of the Earth

After a day of rest and reunions, Lori and I were once again on the trail in the early morning darkness. Lack of daylight made it difficult to find some of the yellow arrows, but we managed not to get lost until later, in full daylight when the sun was brilliant and hot.

I looked back at the city as the eastern sky behind us brightened. The cathedrals spires, wrapped in construction paper, rose against a sky streaked with purple and pink. Below the stunning sky, lights of the city sparkled light jewels against a dark cloth.

Santiago was behind us. The French Camino was finished, but my pilgrimage was not. This Mennonite Apostle had not yet been to the end of the earth.

Almost 90 kilometers beyond Santiago is Finisterre. Or Fisterra. I understand the first spelling is Spanish, the second an English version. But I prefer the first. It still carries the strong Latin roots meaning *the end of the earth.*

This cape and town both bearing the same name are situated on the northwestern corner of Spain, a point that was at one time considered to be the literal end of the earth. Long before Christianity even came into being, this place held great mystery and power—it was the place where the sun came to die. There was nothing beyond this edge of land except the great sea. And thus, many pagan pilgrims came here to offer prayers to the gods for new life and to make sacrifices to appease the deities.

In an interesting irony, this coast is now called *La Casta da Morte,* the Coast of Death. This does not refer to the sun dying but to the death of many ships and sailors who have lost their lives on the dangerous, rocky coast where the Atlantic breaks against the high cliffs.

This is also a Camino route and our path was still marked by yellow arrows and scallop shells. This section is unique in that it is the only Camino route that starts in and leads away from Santiago.

On this first day, the trail led through farm land and quiet, rural Galician villages. It was easy walking. Lori and I hiked about three hours and stopped for coffee and a breakfast pastry. Fewer pilgrims walk this Camino, and we would find that lodging and food was not as easily found as it had been on the way to Santiago.

As we were ready to leave the little café, a couple came around the corner and greeted us, introducing themselves as

Jamie and Christine, a married couple from Canada, who had come to Santiago via a northern route. Their Camino route had started on the northern coast of Spain and was more rugged than the French Camino, had fewer places to stay, and, overall, was a more primitive trail.

We bid each other "Buen Camino!" and off Lori and I went. It wasn't long, however, before Jamie and Christine caught up with us and we hiked together most of the day. The women walked ahead, chatting, and Jamie and I walked together. Somewhere in the conversation, I mentioned I was a Mennonite.

Jamie looked at me and remarked, "I was raised in the Conservative Mennonite Church."

Of all the things I'd heard on the trail, this was probably the biggest surprise. And also a very pleasing surprise. Imagine, hiking toward the end of the earth in Spain and meeting a man from the same kind of background as my own. And he had married a Catholic girl. As you can imagine, Jamie and I had much to discuss as we hiked that day.

We all stayed at the same hostel that evening and found we could sit around the supper table and talk about anything and everything. Meeting these two pilgrims was a special gift. Lori was happy to have a woman to talk with again, and I savored the wonder of meeting someone on this trail who had grown up very much as I had. We had been brought together by the trail, and we shared our journeys and our souls. It was good. Very good.

The guidebook on which we had depended did not take us beyond Santiago. We had heard, though, that the next day's hike to Olveiroa was more desolate with even fewer places to eat and stay.

The path is also not marked as clearly. Leaving town early in heavy fog, Lori and I made a wrong turn and walked a few kilometers before we realized we were no longer on the Camino. A correction—it wasn't that we made a wrong turn. It was that we did not turn when the trail turned; we just went straight ahead.

It was still early in the morning, so no one stopped us and turned us in the right direction. People are very helpful along the trail. Often, you don't even have to ask. Just stop and look confused, and they'll point out the way. The words may be in a language you don't understand, but you'll be sent off in the right direction. At times, someone might even shout at you to tell you you're going the wrong way. These helpful exchanges always end with "Buen Camino" from both sides. You'll hear *Buen Camino* a hundred times a day.

But on this day, no one noticed us going astray. Finally, we realized there were no more markings and we had taken the wrong path. We turned around.

As a result, Jamie and Christine were far ahead of us and we did not see them on the trail that day.

At a breakfast stop, we did meet Angelina, whom we had met several times on the Camino Francés. She was from Germany, and although she spoke English, I preferred to converse with her in German. It felt good to speak in my first language.

Familiar faces were also scarce on this trail, so it was good to occasionally meet and greet any pilgrim who had been a part of our journey from St. Jean to Santiago.

The walk this day was over gently rolling terrain, very scenic and very green.

We found a hostel in Olveiroa, a small town that actually had several albergues. After we checked in, I went in search of Jamie and Christine. They had arrived earlier and were staying at a different hostel. We all gathered for supper and Angelina joined us, along with several other hikers I did not know.

The next day started out well. We hoped to be in Finisterre by that evening. Ascending a hill, we had a view out over a river. A low hanging fog bank had gathered at the river and now made its way up toward us. I stood in awe once again as this ethereal entity moved and flowed across the pathway ahead of us.

Then another formation appeared, one with a more ominous look. Our planned breakfast spot awaited a half mile ahead, but between that place and us hung a grim-looking cloud.

Don't make me dig for my umbrella.

As the first clap of thunder sounded, a frustrated yell also came from my hiking partner.

"I left my bag with all my money and ID back at the hostel."

"Are you sure?" I asked. If there is anything a pilgrim wants to avoid, it is having to turn around and go back.

Lori was certain. She always kept the bag at the same place on her backpack. Now it was not there. She remembered attaching it to the frame of her bunk the night before. She knew precisely where she had attached it and recalled that she forgotten to remove it.

"I'll wait for you at the café just up ahead."

With that, she was off and running. This was a gear I had not seen her use before this day. I believe that gear was marked *panic and adrenalin*.

A short while later, I walked into the small café as the first customer of the day. My arrival was synchronized perfectly with the arrival of the rain.

Perhaps I could have offered to take Lori's pack so that she could run lighter—but then she would have been without rain gear.

Soon Angelina arrived at the café with Martin, another familiar face from our trek to Santiago. They reported that they had met Lori running in the opposite direction and that she had stopped and donned her rain gear. I explained her backward flight.

An hour passed and we remained warm and dry. Another hour passed, and finally Lori arrived, tired and wet but smiling. She had found her valuables at the same spot she had placed them the night before.

We waited in the café until the rain stopped and then hiked on. The hills were growing, getting larger and steeper. The scenery was beginning to remind me of the hills of my own county back home. In the distance, the hills became mountains.

A bit farther along, we had a choice to make. There is that proverbial fork in the road where one must decide. One road led to the right, headed toward Muxia. The other went left, to Finisterre. We had already made our choice; we were going to Finisterre first, then to Muxia. It is possible to visit the two towns in reverse order, but those in their right mind went left.
    The trail grew steeper in places and was sometimes rocky. As we wound around the hillsides that were beginning to feel like mountainsides, we caught our first views of the Atlantic Ocean and the land once thought to be the end of the earth.

35

Finisterre

Finisterre is a fishing town. Boats were moored in the harbor. White buildings are topped with red roofs, and the little town is cupped between green hills and brilliant blue water. Along the edges of the water are several white sand beaches. It's a postcard-perfect setting.

Here I collected another compostela. This actually brought the number in my collection to three. In Santiago I had received one that is awarded only once in a century. I happened to be on the Camino in that one year when these compostelas were issued. I would collect one more—in Muxia, the absolute, final end of the road.

An absolutely essential walk for pilgrims is the 3-kilometer hike to Faro de Finisterre, the lighthouse sitting at the edge of a cliff overlooking the Coast of Death. Many pilgrims end their journey here. As usual, a stone cross rose from one boulder. We found permanent memorials carved in stone and makeshift memorials left by pilgrims—shells and rocks left by crosses or piled in cairns, pieces of clothing or shoes hung on a tower, and as always, some graffiti.

Over hundreds of years, pilgrims have arrived here after long, difficult journeys. Traditions evolved, some of which are still observed today. They arrived filthy and stinking, and in rituals that were both practical and symbolic, they would burn their clothing and jump into the ocean to cleanse themselves. It was an outer and inner cleansing, a baptism of sorts. The traditions evolved and are still observed today. Some folks burn clothes in a pit on the cliff, next to a stone cross. Although I do like to follow tradition, I could not part with my shoes, and I'm emotionally attached to my North Face pants—it would pain me to throw those in the fire. And what about my cleansing in the ocean? Was I going to follow that tradition?

It was still under consideration.

When we returned from the lighthouse, Lori and I were eating by the waterfront and discussing hiking on to Muxia. A young lady sitting alone overheard our conversation. She had turned right at the sign and gone to Muxia first, and she shared with us what she had learned about accommodations along the way.

"Where have I seen you before?" I inquired. Lori was much better than I at remembering names and places we had met people.

Ah yes, she was the girl we had met back in Bayonne while we waited to catch the train to St. Jean. Her name was Alexandra, and she was taking a year off and traveling the world. We had not seen her since that train ride. Interestingly, she had actually started the Camino the same day we had, but somehow our paths had never crossed—except here, at the end of the earth. She mentioned that she had walked from Santiago with a young lady named Judit. Ah, my friend Judit! I was happy to know that I would get to see her once again.

We saw a few other familiar faces in town. On the waterfront, I caught a glimpse of the mysterious tall Asian man with the guitar. Again, he was only carrying it. I never saw him playing it. As I strolled about town, I saw Martin in a café and sat down to talk with him, and, shortly, in walked my dark-eyed friend Judit and joined us.

It is the people who make our pilgrimages joyous.

36

Muxia

Lori and I hiked the additional 30 kilometers to Muxia the next day. We left a sleepy Finisterre at dawn and followed the coastline for miles, walking along the cliffs. This is also a section of the Camino, and the scallop shell markers still led us onward.

We also saw more of the giant, repulsive slugs. And more of the granaries. These were constructed entirely of stone, impressive in design and distinctively Galician. I could not resist teasing Lori.

"Did you see that spirit house filled with corn to feed the spirits?"

Far more likely, I thought to myself, *that it's corn to make spirits.*

The stone crosses that appear at so many places were becoming a symbol of Galicia to me. Sheep and cattle are also a part of the pictures that linger in my mind. In one town, we happened on the running of the sheep. A small flock came down the main street as we walked into the village. The shepherd followed them, leading a donkey and cart.

In Muxia, I posed beside another marker, this one simply bearing the road number and telling travelers *km 0*. The road literally ends here in Muxia.

We visited Muxia's lighthouse and a stone chapel and took in the sights. Away from all other eyes, I found a deserted, pristine beach, and there I observed the tradition of washing off my pilgrim dirt in the waters of the ocean. It was too cold, though, and the ritual amounted to a dashing in and out again rather quickly.

Drawn to the waterfront in Muxia, I was walking along the harbor at dusk, making my way back to our albergue. I followed a circuitous route, deep in thought.

This would be my last night sleeping in a hostel. I'd had so many neat encounters with folks from all over the world. The memories of occasional less-than-happy occurrences that arise when one lives with the masses were hiding in the back corner of my mind that evening.

I have never liked endings, and this special hike and time of my life was now truly coming to an end. I had walked to the end of the earth.

I almost bumped into the stranger standing at the edge of the sidewalk and admiring the views.

"A fine night it is, isn't it?" spoke the stranger.

"Yes, beautiful," I replied.

We introduced ourselves and talk turned to occupations. He was a priest from Our Land. At least, that's the way it sounded to my ears. His Irish accent transformed *Ireland* to *Our Land*.

So he was *Father* Mike, then.

He told me of being robbed in Santiago. His money and passport were stolen. When he reported the theft to the police and they discovered he was a priest, they had put him in contact with the cathedral authorities, and his passport was mysteriously recovered. Through this contact with the cathedral, Father Mike was also given an invitation to do an English mass when he returned to Santiago.

An English mass. In all the time I'd been in Spain, I had not had the opportunity to be in a service conducted in a language I understood (no, they did not have a Pennsylvania Dutch service either), and I really didn't have much of an idea of what was going on.

But what if Father Mike and I were back in Santiago at the same time? What if he had an English mass and this Mennonite fellow just happened to show up, and what if Father Mike did not make that ominous statement barring non-Catholics from communion?

The following day we boarded a bus back to Santiago. It was an odd sensation to be speeding along and passing hikers headed to Finisterre. Jamie and Christine had walked to Muxia the day before Lori and I, and they were now walking back to Santiago. We would reunite back in the city before we all headed home.

Back in Santiago, Lori and I checked into our rooms on the fourth floor of an old monastery just off the cathedral's plaza. The first three floors had been renovated as an upscale hotel, and the fourth floor was reserved for pilgrims. For a modest price, we each had a small, private room. My room looked out over the cathedral.

I had two days left before my flight home. For the first time since leaving Paris, I was alone. I wandered around town, visiting markets, admiring the old buildings, and purchasing gifts for the grandkids.

Watching new pilgrims arrive, I felt a strange mixture of emotions. I knew none of them, recognized no faces, and my story had no connection at all with theirs.

Oh, but I did recognize two faces. Nick finally arrived in Santiago and Simon was also in town now too. Nick had connected with some other young men, and they decided to walk on to Finisterre. Simon had connected with a woman, and they were together in Santiago. He looked haggard, though, as if he were not well. We had supper with him one night.

For the most part, I was just waiting. Waiting to go home.

But there is one more very important thing that occurred during that time in Santiago that I must tell you about.

37

Pilgrim Communion

When I checked in at the monastery hotel, a sign posted at the main entrance caught my eye. It announced that an English mass would be conducted at the cathedral at 10:30 the following day.

Could it possibly be Father Mike conducting that mass? There was only one way to find out.

The following morning, Lori and I arrived at the cathedral by 10:15. I didn't want to miss the chance to get a good seat. A small scattering of people mingled about. At the appointed time, no mass occurred and the crowd had not grown. I waited a while, then decided to ask a man in uniform about the

English mass. He informed me that it was being held in a side chapel adjacent to the main cathedral. And it had already started.

The chapel was crowded and overflowing with pilgrims when I entered. A gentleman standing by the door handed me a leaflet and informed me I would need to stand in the aisle since all seats were filled. I glanced at the leaflet. It was an outline of "The Order of Mass" *in English.*

Father Mike was at the altar, already speaking. My entrance caused enough of a distraction that he noticed me. In the middle of a sentence, he paused, and in that beautiful Irish brogue said, "Welcome, Paul."

Every head tuned to see who Welcome Paul was, and to their amazement, Welcome Paul returned the greeting with "Hello, Father Mike."

From discussions with Padre, I knew that a homily is the equivalent of our sermon. Father Mike was in the middle of the homily. He was drawing examples from the Camino journey to illustrate spiritual lessons of the Christian walk in life.

He spoke about how the trail wore down hikers physically and mentally. After a while, our bodies become broken down, too. When we are broken down, then we can be broken open. Like the alabaster box holding precious perfume, we are broken open to worship and serve Christ. Perhaps after we get broken down and broken open, the aroma is not so pleasant for a while. The Holy Spirit works at that, burning our old, stinky stuff and turning us into a better aroma.

I have been broken open. Broken open to release my judgmental attitudes. In my very first book, I wrote of praying in a Catholic church, and at that time it seemed a very strange thing for a Conservative Mennonite boy to be doing. Eventually, Padre came hiking along the trail and into my life, with his flute and floppy hat. Then came David and his one-word sermon on faith. Then came an Irish priest who would feed a hunger in my soul. Some of the deepest lessons I've learned about following Jesus have come through my Catholic friends, and a very Catholic trail has challenged me to ponder Scriptures that I've glossed over and downplayed before.

Father Mike also quoted a line that John Brierley included in the Camino guidebook: "When you meet anyone, remember it is a holy encounter. And as you see *them* you will see *yourself.*" (from *A Course in Miracles*, Helen Schucman)

From the first steps of the AT hike, I have believed that God has scheduled appointments for me along my path in life. But I must remember as I meet other pilgrims that I am meeting other sons and daughters of God.

"As we walk through towns and villages," said Father Mike, "we're Jesus to the people we meet. We are Christ in disguise."

I am still asking Jesus to show me more of what it means to be His disciple. Unknowingly, when I first set foot on the Appalachian Trail, I chose a trail name that seems to have shaped my life and pilgrimage. Or perhaps the Holy Spirit did the choosing for me, and thus sent me off on my mission, a mission to be carried out in the towns and villages I walk through for the rest of my life.

On my "Order of Mass" leaflet I scrawled more thoughts prompted by the homily that day in Santiago. But I can no longer decipher my scribbles. I've turned the paper every which way, and still can't determine what I wrote. It looks like *Under head afro hes of ache.*

My apologies. Neither you nor I will ever know what that profound thought might have been.

After the homily came a time of reflection. This is something more of our churches could use, a time to let the words and the Word soak into our bones.

Then came a profession of faith by the congregation.

> "I believe in one God,
> the Father almighty,
> maker of heaven and earth,
> of all things visible and invisible.
> I believe in one Lord Jesus Christ...
> for our sake he was crucified...
> was buried...
> rose again...
> and will come again in glory to judge the living and the dead
> and his kingdom will have no end.
> I believe in the Holy Spirit, the Lord, the giver of life..."

Most of the words came easily to this Mennonite tongue and mind, because this is my faith, too.

A prayer followed.

When my eyes opened again, my heartbeat quickened. The next thing on the leaflet was "The Liturgy of the Eucharist."

While an offering was taken, the bread and wine were brought forward. There were prayers of blessing from the priest, including these words:

> "May the Lord accept the sacrifice at your hands
> for the praise and glory of his name,
> for our good
> and the good of all his holy Church."

The Lord's holy church, I thought, *is comprised of many unholy people.* I felt a gentle correction. The Lord's holy church is comprised of all us unholy Mennonites and Catholics (and everyone else in between) who *have been made holy* by the body and blood of Christ, this sacrifice *He* has made for *our* good.

We prayed the Lord's Prayer. The same prayer I have prayed all my life in my Mennonite church. One prayer to one Lord.

When the priest addressed the audience with "Let us offer one another the customary sign of peace," all around me folks shook hands, some gave kisses on cheeks, and everyone said to each other, "Peace be with you." *Buen Camino.*

Finally ready for what we call the breaking of the bread, Father Mike raised the host. I thought of Christ being lifted up on the cross.

The body of Christ. The blood of Christ.

After Father Mike, the congregation was invited to come forward and partake of communion. Those are probably the Mennonite words, not the Catholic words. This service was so familiar, so much like our own, that as I was following the Catholic liturgy my mind was translating everything into Mennonite terminology. It's something like speaking Dutch with a liberal amount of English words scattered throughout the discourse without consciously thinking about switching from one language to another.

But—had I heard correctly? I *had not heard* the dreaded announcement. Perhaps it would still be made. I waited. No. No announcement. Perhaps because this was an English mass, it was assumed folks would know the correct protocol.

Perhaps this priest had no concerns about heathen Mennonites... perhaps, perhaps. A lot of perhapses, but the only thing I knew for certain was that no announcement had been made.

I got in line. And partook.

And what of the cup from which we all drank, that detail of communion that had always caused me such consternation?

I drank. With many other pilgrims, I shared fully in commemorating and celebrating the death that gave me life.

And it was wonderful.

Father Mike's eyes met mine briefly. Did I imagine it, or did he give me a slight nod?

Or was it perhaps a nod of approval from Jesus over these two pilgrims who had met and communed together on the trail?

"The Concluding Rites" included hymns and announcements. We were dismissed with a reiteration of Christ's words to every one of His followers: "We are sent out to fulfill in our daily lives our mission to witness to Christ in the world."

I left the cathedral and walked back to my room. At the Gate of the Way in the old wall, an opera singer now greeted pilgrims with a majestic melody whose words I could not understand. The notes followed me all the way back to the monastery.

Later that evening I had supper with Jamie and Christine. Since he had at one time been a Mennonite and she was a Catholic, we had discussed many things in the few days we had together. In one particular conversation, we had compared the Catholic belief in transubstantiation to the Mennonites' beliefs about the celebration of communion.

That evening, I tried to describe to them how special that day's communion had been to me. I also told them how repulsed I used to be by drinking from the same cup as everyone else.

Christine looked at me with a sly grin.

"It can't hurt you. It's the blood of Christ."

38

Bones Dead and Alive

I visited the relics while I was in Santiago.

Did those around me know that it was a Mennonite black sheep standing in line, waiting his turn to have a few moments with the bones of James the Greater?

Whether you can understand the reverence given to the bones of an apostle or not, there can be no question that deep faith is what brings many pilgrims here. And to those pilgrims, the relics of St. James are revered.

Inside the cathedral, a narrow, steep stairway leads to a small crypt under the altar. Here, the bones of St. James lie in a silver coffin. Only a handful of folks can enter the crypt at one time, reflect and pray for a few moments, and then climb the stairs and exit. The line was long, and I waited my turn.

In the light of flickering candles, one man knelt in front of the casket and wept. I realized the power of this journey we had all undertaken. I did not know this man's story or what brought the tears, but I understood his emotion as I was transported back to my own kneeling and weeping at the sign on Mt. Katahdin.

Some question these bones. Whether they are the remains of James the follower of Jesus Christ or those of some wandering sheep herder, these bones do have power. Over the centuries, they have drawn millions of pilgrims from all over the world to a place called the Field of Stars. Folks have faced famine and death attempting to reach those bones.

Yes, dead bones can have power. In the Old Testament we read a story about the power of dead bones.

The prophet Elisha took the mantle from Elijah and went on to do great things. He healed a young boy by lying atop him until the boy revived. He did that with his vibrant live bones. (See Chapter 4 of the second book of Kings.)

Elisha died and they buried him. One spring, Moabite raiders arrived, as they were wont to do. The timing was inconvenient for one community; mourners were in the middle of a funeral procession. The timing, however, was perfect for one other fellow—the dead dude. He had to be one of the most fortunate dead people ever.

In panic and haste as the Moabites attacked, the mourners unceremoniously tossed the body into the tomb where Elisha's body had been interred. Only a skeleton remained. However, those relics still contained power. As soon as that corpse landed on Elisha's dry bones, the man was immediately zapped back to life. You have to admit, it does make you rethink all those doubts about power in relics.

My Catholic friends of deep faith believe that Saint Iago still cares for pilgrims along the way to the Field of Stars. I've heard and read many stories of miracles that seem to support that faith. What do I believe? I don't have a clear answer to that question yet.

But there is another question every follower of Jesus must contemplate: What about our live bones? Are these live bones meant to care for those on pilgrimage?

James the Pilgrim began his journey when Jesus called him from a fisherman's life. When Jesus calls His followers to a life of following Him, He makes some promises about imbuing our living bones with power.

Until we meet again in my next book or somewhere else along the journey, ask Him about those promises and ponder His answer.

One thing is certain. All of us who follow Jesus have these instructions from Him: "Love each other. Just as I have loved you, you should love each other. And your love will prove to the world you are My disciples."

I meet many pilgrims on the road. Most do not look like me and may not worship as I do and each has had many different experiences along the trail. But we have one common goal. We have set our sights and our hearts on that heavenly country where we now have our citizenship and where homes are being prepared for us.

The Jesus we follow says, *Along the way, love your fellow pilgrims as I love you.*

Buen Camino.

After the Camino

If you enjoyed *Pilgrims,* a positive review on Amazon.com would help to spread the message.

Now that we have that bit of commercialism out of the way, here are a few more words to you, my much-appreciated readers.

I arrived home from Spain the same day an aunt was buried. Two days later, I attended the funeral service of an uncle who had passed away. He had lived 92 years. Several months later, another uncle, aged 100, passed on to his reward.

Sitting in those services, I was reminded of that sunflower field in Spain where I wept as I recognized the great blessings of my heritage.

My father recently turned 90, but his heath is declining rapidly. He and these other great warriors of faith set their minds on pilgrimage at an early age. Each person's pilgrimage begins at the moment of birth, but how you set your mind determines *where* you will arrive, and the Bible tells us there are two vastly different destinations.

On our pilgrimage, we will pass through numerous valleys of weeping. Keeping our eyes set on the final destination gives us the courage to soldier on. In these valleys of weeping, strength from the Lord is promised and His blessings will come like the rain to refresh our journey.

And when our path does take us through these valleys, we have a choice in what our lives will be—whether we will allow the weeping to shape us or whether we will look for the promised strength and blessings. The desert valley can be watered with refreshing springs.

I have learned that cancer did not shape my life; my choices shaped my life. Cancer happened *to* me and my wife. What happens to us might send our feet down a detour we never wished to take. Yet even in the valleys, we have choices and it is those choices that truly shape our us and our future paths.

Folks often ask me what I'm planning for my next adventure. On my Camino hike, I tried to grasp more of what it meant to be a follower of Jesus. I imagined this from the perspective of the Apostle James as he followed Jesus so closely that he heard and pursued this assignment: Take the message to the ends of the earth.

Every day I look for more insight into what it means for me to be a disciple of Jesus. Now I'm contemplating a trip to Israel where I hope to learn more.

Another question has entered my awareness. In John 5:25 Jesus says that folks in their graves will hear His voice and those who listen will live. I can't explain dead people hearing any voices at all, but I do hear Jesus saying that those who listen to Him will have eternal life. I want to be sure I hear Him—*before* I'm in my grave. As we seek to follow Him, how do we hear what He has to say to us? How do we listen for God speaking to us? If I'm at the back of the flock, can I still hear

His voice? Jesus talked a lot about doing good, but what is "doing good" according to Him? What the disciple James heard as he followed Jesus changed the direction of his life. How do we know what Jesus is saying to His modern-day disciples?

If plans to visit Israel do come to fruition, my hope is that Jesus will teach me, too, as He walks with me along the same hills, valleys, and lakeshores that He and James hiked together.

My prayer for you, my friend, is that your heart is also set on pilgrimage—a pilgrimage with a destination leading to eternal bliss.

And just as the Good Samaritan did in a parable Jesus taught, I encourage you to help fellow pilgrims you meet along the way.

His disciples are to be Jesus to others.

Paul Stutzman

GET TO KNOW PAUL STUTZMAN at
www.paulstutzman.com
www.facebook.com/pvstutzman
pstutzman@roadrunner.com

OTHER BOOKS BY PAUL STUTZMAN
The Wandering Home Series (Fiction)
Book One: The Wanderers
Book Two: Wandering Home
Book Three: Wander No More

Adventure Memoir
Hiking Through
  One Man's Journey to Peace and Freedom on the Appalachian Trail
Biking Across America
  My Coast-to-Coast Adventure and the People I Met Along the Way
Mississippi Misadventure
  (Formerly a section of *Stuck in the Weeds*)
Hiking Israel (Also available under the title *The 13th Disciple*)
  From Galilee to Jerusalem

Spiritual Memoir
Don't Wait Too Long
The Miracle Journey:
  Guideposts to Restoration after Heartbreak and Loss

With Author Serena Miller
More Than Happy: The Wisdom of Amish Parenting

"Young fella, where you frum? Why you running away?"

Leroy L. Jackson, Jr. detected it immediately. Others could see it, too, even if Johnny Miller wouldn't admit it. He was running. Whether he was running from home or toward home, he did not know.

Johnny Miller was twenty-three when he died the first time. The truck hit him as he pedaled along a Texas road, biking across the country in an attempt to find, somehow, somewhere, a new life.

His old life had vanished like a vapor. He thought he had lost everything on the day he lost his dear Annie. But he will lose far more before finally finding the way that leads to home... and life and peace.

Johnny Miller is back home again, farming the land he loves in a quiet Amish community in Ohio. But although he's not physically wandering, he is still wondering. Wondering why he is restless. Wondering why he feels that some piece of his life is not yet in place. Wondering why, when he was medically "dead," he was met by his wife, who told him his time to enter Heaven had not yet come—he was still needed on earth.

After Paul Stutzman lost his wife to breast cancer, he sensed a tug on his heart—the call to pursue a dream. Paul left his stable career, traveled to Georgia, and took his first steps on the Appalachian Trail. What he learned during the next four and a half months on the trail changed his life—and will change readers' lives as well.

Paul Stutzman trades his hiking boots for a bicycle and sets off from Neah Bay, Washington, ending in Key West, Florida, traversing 5,000 miles. Along the way, he encounters nearly every kind of terrain and weather the country has to offer—as well as fascinating people whose stories readers will love.

"Imprisoned in my kayak, I leaned back and wondered if this choice I had made was perhaps the most foolish, ill-advised choice of my entire life." Attempting to kayak the length of the Mississippi River, Paul re-thinks his choices and his spiritual journey. (Previously published as a segment of *Stuck in the Weeds*)

On a hike through Israel, Paul Stutzman and his friend Craig visit places that were prominent in the life and ministry of Jesus. Paul is seeking two things: to better know the human Jesus and to find the answer to a question that has puzzled him for years: What does it mean to follow Jesus? (Also found under the title *The 13th Disciple*)

In a deeply personal reflection, Paul writes about two love stories during two years of his life. Don't postpone dreams. Don't wait until the perfect "someday." Paul's message is urgent and applicable to your walk of faith and your human relationships.

COMING IN 2021:

The Miracle Journey:
Guideposts to Restoration after Heartbreak and Loss

"This book is not for everyone," Paul says emphatically. Following his own heartbreak and deep loss, Paul writes to those who have experienced devastation in their lives—loss of loved ones, betrayals, loss of dreams, catastrophic illness or disaster. How do you survive after life has been shattered? More than that, how is it possible to once again flourish and find hope and joy? Paul invites you along on this spiritual journey as he looks for the miracle.

Author Serena B. Miller talks with Amish parents to discover principles of parenting and family life in Amish homes. Paul Stutzman contributes from his own Amish and Conservative Mennonite upbringing.

With practical takeaways for every family—regardless of religion—on how to raise happy, responsible, productive kids.

www.ingramcontent.com/pod-product-compliance
Lightning Source LLC
Chambersburg PA
CBHW071306110426
42743CB00042B/1190